PSYCHOLOGY

50 IDEAS IN 500 WORDS

This edition published in Great Britain, Australia and New Zealand in
2018 by Modern Books

An imprint of Elwin Street Productions Limited
14 Clerkenwell Green
London EC1R 0DP
www.modern-books.com

All illustrations by Joanna Kerr, except for page 45. All icons and the
illustration on page 45 by Emma Farrarons.

ISBN 978-1-911130-74-1

10 9 8 7 6 5 4 3 2 1

Printed in Poland

PSYCHOLOGY

50 IDEAS IN 500 WORDS

JEREMY STANGROOM

Contents

The Social Animal

In Sickness and in Health

Introduction

The word 'psychology', derived from the Greek words 'psyche' (soul or mind) and 'logos' (knowledge or study), means literally 'the study of the mind'. Although the term first gained general usage in the eighteenth century, it wasn't until the end of the nineteenth century that it began to be used in its modern sense to refer to a distinct domain of enquiry that aims at the scientific understanding of human thought and behaviour.

In the present day, under the rubric of psychology, researchers investigate phenomena as diverse as learning, perception, attention, memory, personality, ageing, prejudice, obedience, mental illness and human flourishing. In this book, we'll touch on all these topics through the ideas and work of fifty of the greatest psychologists ever to have lived, each one of whom has made a significant contribution to the body of knowledge that constitutes modern psychology.

The history of psychology is in large part the history of its great experiments, and this is reflected in the pages to follow. We're interested in psychology as a living, breathing endeavour, in the research that led to breakthroughs in our understanding of mind and behaviour.

The most famous of these experiments have influenced not only the discipline of psychology, but also the zeitgeist of modern life. Thus, Peter Gabriel sings about Milgram's obedience studies in 'We Do What We're Told', the last track on his multimillion selling album, *So*; and in 2002, the BBC replicated Zimbardo's Stanford Prison Experiment, broadcasting the results in *The Experiment*, a documentary series that ran for five episodes in May of that year.

The extent to which academic psychology is now part of our wider culture has been demonstrated over the last several years by the attention given to what has been called its replication crisis. An experiment is scientific, and its findings are considered robust, if it is possible to replicate its methodology, and generate the same results. The replication crisis emerged after a group of psychological researchers failed to replicate hundreds of previously published studies. The reasons why are complex, and the extent to which the replication crisis is a real problem is open to debate, but the issue has been extensively covered in the mainstream press.

In a strong sense, this is indicative of the health of psychology as a relevant and vital domain of intellectual enquiry. Its results matter. Science is self-correcting, and the best research is always revisable in the light of new findings and criticism. A living science does not ossify in a complacent acceptance of its established truths, but rather seeks new and innovative ways to get to the bottom of things.

It is often the case that psychologists, like most of us, live unremarkable lives, and their legacy to the discipline lies solely in the body of research they bequeath to their colleagues. But there are exceptions. The luminaries in the field – James, Freud, Jung – led remarkable lives, and conjured up ideas and theories that have had a far-reaching cultural and social impact, changing the way we see ourselves and our place in the world. These few rare geniuses stand out, not because their prominence diminishes the importance of their less celebrated colleagues, but because their ideas and work exemplify how the concerns of psychology have an abiding human significance.

Jeremy Stangroom

From Beginnings to Behavioural

The discipline of psychology had its
beginnings in the nineteenth century
as the human mind increasingly
came to be seen as an object
worthy of systematic study. In this
section, we consider the work of
early introspective psychologists
such as Wilhelm Wundt and trace
the emergence of psychology as
a distinct field of inquiry through
the ideas of the first behaviourist
psychologists.

The Birth of a Science

Psychology as the behaviourist views it is a purely objective experimental branch of natural science. Its theoretical goal is the prediction and control of behaviour.

John B. Watson

Human beings have been interested in the workings of the mind for almost as long as they have been documenting their interest in anything. The ancient Greek philosopher Aristotle, for example, wrote a treatise on the psyche (or soul), in which he discussed, among other things, the character of sense experience, thinking and the imagination.

However, until modern times, discussion of the mind tended to be highly speculative in character, and was generally considered to fall under the remit of philosophy. The emergence of psychology as a distinct discipline occurred only in the latter part of the nineteenth century, with the opening of Wilhelm Wundt's psychological laboratory in 1879 and with the concomitant drive to put the investigation of the mind on a scientific footing.

Wundt and his colleagues employed the technique of introspection, which took place in a laboratory setting and careful efforts were made to ensure that extraneous variables, such as delivered instructions and the character of a given stimulus (for example, the ticking of a metronome), were held constant. In this way, they hoped the results of introspection would be unaffected by the particular setting in which an experiment took place and would accurately reflect the structure of conscious experience.

But their method of psychology was not as scientific as the Wundtians might have hoped. The problem was that the technique of introspection does not produce objective, replicable results. If two researchers trained in introspection employ the technique in order to discern how they experience the ticking of a metronome, and then get different results, there is no way of telling who is right. Introspection, by its very nature, is bound up with individual subjectivity and, therefore, cannot be the grounds upon which a reliable body of knowledge is built.

By the first decade of the twentieth century, rumblings about the unreliability of the technique were beginning to be heard. In particular, the American psychologist John B. Watson was scathing about introspection. The Wundtian orthodoxy began to crumble in 1913 with the publication of Watson's article, 'Psychology as the Behaviourist Views It', in which he argued that psychology should concern itself only with observable behaviour. If psychology wanted to put itself on an equal footing with natural science, then it had to replicate the rigour of its methods, which meant concentrating on what could be observed and measured, and abandoning all references to the internal realm of private experiences.

Thus, Watson defined psychology as 'that division of Natural Science which takes human behaviour – the doings and sayings, both learned and unlearned – as its subject matter'.

In the battle between Wundtian introspectionism and Watsonian behaviourism, the latter decisively won the day. Behaviourism quickly became the dominant psychological paradigm for studying human behaviour, particularly in North America, and remained so for nearly 50 years. It was only with the emergence of cognitive psychology in the 1950s that behaviourism's dominance began to be challenged.

Pierre Cabanis

After training as a doctor of medicine, Pierre Cabanis rose to prominence in late eighteenth-century France as a member of the Ideologues, a group of thinkers committed to the possibility of a 'science of man'.

Born: 1757, Cosnac, France
Importance: Argued that thoughts and ideas are determined by the senses
Died: 1808, Meulan-en-Yvelines, France

Cabanis's signature work, *On the Relations Between the Physical and Moral Aspects of Man*, argues for a broadly materialist understanding of the relationship between mind and body. He believed that biological life is partly distinguished by its ability to have sensations, and that all our thoughts, feelings and ideas are caused by sensations. Thus, he was well known for his comparison between the brain and the stomach, arguing that just as the stomach is a machine for digesting food, so the brain is a machine for digesting sense impressions or, as he put it, secreting thought.

Cabanis is by no means a modern figure. Towards the end of his magnum opus, for example, he discusses the issue of how much water a person absorbs while bathing, arguing that the amount is linked to a person's temperament: the less phlegmatic they are, the more water they're going to absorb.

He also suggested that the chemical phosphorus was central to the functioning of the nervous system, justifying this claim in part by noting that a deceased brain on a dissection table gives off a phosphoric glow. Moreover, he claimed that if a person died of a disease characterized by an excess of brain activity, there would be a brighter and more vivid light after death – the brains of 'maniacs' are very bright; those of phlegmatics much less so.

Cabanis's thoughts about the functioning of the nervous system were not entirely speculative. He was aware of Benjamin Franklin's experiments with electricity and accepted Luigi Galvani's contention that muscular activity is produced by the electrical activity of the nervous system. But even here his understanding was premodern, as evidenced by his claim that the electrical 'fluid' that animates living bodies behaves differently from the electricity studied by scientists in their laboratories.

Others of his concerns, however, are more recognizably modern. He espouses a version of the (erroneous) idea that organisms evolve by means of the inheritance of acquired characteristics, and he favours a programme of selective breeding to improve the human condition. He posits the existence of an unconscious, which makes its presence felt during dreams (thereby anticipating one of Freud's central ideas). And he rejects the 'blank slate' view of human nature, which holds that whatever one finds in the mind has come in from the outside, stressing instead the importance of internal physiological factors such as age, sex, bodily 'dispositions' and health.

Materialism: The view that the only thing that exists is physical matter, and that all phenomena, including consciousness, are ultimately reducible to matter.

The work of Cabanis is now only of historical interest. Nevertheless, his attempt to understand the human mind in terms of the workings of an underlying physiology was an important moment in the early development of the science that eventually became psychology.

Francis Galton

The nineteenth-century polymath Francis Galton is probably best known for his advocacy of eugenics – in his terms, the science that 'deals with all the influences that improve the inborn qualities of the [human] race'. In a sense, this is unfortunate, because his association with the eugenics movement and its deadly history has tainted what is in fact a rich intellectual legacy.

Born: 1822, Birmingham, England
Importance: Devised the first intelligence tests
Died: 1911, Haslemere, England

In the field of psychology, Galton pioneered the study of individual differences, in particular creating the first recognizable tests of intelligence. To learn something about memory, he developed a technique of word association. He was the first to make systematic use of questionnaires, and created a number of new statistical techniques that enabled him to interrogate his data more precisely. And he had novel opinions about such things as mental imagery, inheritance and nature versus nurture.

The tests of intelligence devised by Galton seem rather bizarre by today's standards. They rest on the assumption that a person's overall mental ability will be correlated with their sensory acuity. So, for example, he devised a test to determine how accurately people were able to discriminate between different weights, and another one to measure the ability to detect pitch. In 1882, Galton established a testing centre in London, where, for a fee, a person could take a series of such tests and receive a report at the end.

> There were no satisfactory ways of measuring the strength of association between characteristics until Galton.
>
> Harvey Goldstein, *On the Relations Between the Physical and Moral Aspects of Man*

Above: Word association was a research technique in Galton's arsenal of intelligence tests. He would ask patients to confirm typical associations: if I say 'cat', you might say 'paw'. This would indicate a common association.

Galton's most famous test of mental imagery involved asking his subjects to conjure up the picture of their breakfast table that morning, and then to report on whether it was clear, detailed, in colour and so on. To his surprise, he found that there was considerable variation in this ability, a result confirmed by the research of later psychologists.

Galton's importance in the history of psychology should not be underestimated. Although he did not inspire a legion of followers in the same way that Wundt did, above anybody else he showed how psychologists could fruitfully explore the differences between individuals.

Eugenics: The science, pioneered by Francis Galton, that aims to improve the genetic stock of the human species by means of selective breeding.

Wilhelm Wundt

Wilhelm Wundt is properly regarded as the founder of the science of psychology. In 1864, he taught the first course in 'Physiological Psychology' at the University of Heidelberg; in 1874, his groundbreaking *Principles of Physiological Psychology* was published; and five years later, he established the world's first experimental psychology laboratory at the University of Leipzig.

Born: 1832, Manheim, Germany
Importance: Pioneered the practice of introspection as a formal discipline
Died: 1920, Großbothen, Germany

Wundt believed that the new science of psychology should aim at uncovering the fundamental structures of conscious thought, arguing that the technique best suited to this task was introspection, the process of examining the contents of one's own mind. However, he did not mean the kind of introspection that we all practise in our daily lives, but rather a rigorous, controlled version of it, designed to elicit reliable knowledge about the human mind.

Wundt's general approach can be illustrated with reference to a series of experiments he conducted with a metronome. A standard experiment would involve a highly trained subject, normally one of Wundt's students, focusing their attention on a carefully selected series of clicks, and then reporting back on some particular aspect of their experience – whether they had experienced the clicks disparately or as a unified whole, for example. It would then be possible to vary the speed and rhythm of the metronome to see whether that had an effect on the experience.

> The distinguishing characteristics of mind are of a subjective sort; we know them only from the contents of our own consciousness.
>
> *Principles of Physiological Psychology*

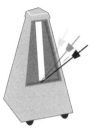

pleasantness - unpleasantness   relaxation - tension   calm - excitement

Above: It was through Wundt's series of experiments with metronomes that he found he experienced three different emotions depending on the speed of their beats, and thus came to believe in his tridimensional theory of feeling.

It was in the light of his own experiments with a metronome that Wundt developed his tridimensional theory of feeling. He noted that he tended to experience three different kinds of reaction to the metronome: pleasure and displeasure depending on its rhythm; relaxation and tension depending on whether he was waiting for an anticipated click to occur; and calm or excitement depending on the speed of its beat. On the basis of repeated listenings, therefore, he concluded that every conscious feeling will vary along three continuums: pleasantness-unpleasantness, relaxation-tension and calm-excitement.

Psychologists no longer take Wundt's theory of feeling seriously, but, nevertheless, his place in the history of psychology is assured.

William James

William James is in many ways a contradictory figure. He was reluctant to call himself a psychologist yet wrote one of the classics of the discipline. He largely eschewed applied research but established the first psychology laboratory on the American continent. He believed in the importance of the scientific method yet was sympathetic to spiritualism and a founding member of the American Society for Psychical Research. He is probably better known in the present day as a philosopher, and particularly for his advocacy of 'pragmatism', but nobody seriously doubts that he is one of the most important psychologists ever to have lived.

Born: 1842, New York, New York
Importance: Highly influential in defining consciousness as flux
Died: 1910, Tamworth, New Hampshire

James argued that the starting point of psychology is thought or consciousness. However, he rejected the Wundtian idea that consciousness can be broken down into discrete foundational elements – feelings and sensations – arguing instead that it has five distinct characteristics.

First, every thought is necessarily personal, it belongs to somebody. Thus, James argued that the most fundamental conscious fact is that *I* think and *I* feel.

Consciousness is also in constant flux, which means that we can never have the same conscious thought or be in the same conscious state more than once. This point is shown most clearly by the fact that different objects will conjure up quite different thoughts and emotions depending on our mood, the passage of time and so on.

A third characteristic of consciousness is that it is experienced as a continuous flow, and not as being chopped into little bits. James was aware that there are breaks in consciousness, of course, but argued that the fact that we so easily reconnect with our own conscious past after such a break – perhaps upon waking from sleep, for example – demonstrates its continuous character.

Another attribute of consciousness is that it is necessarily discriminating and selective. We grasp particular aspects of objects by means of a process of emphasizing, accepting, rejecting and unifying. We do not merely attend passively to the totality of our experience.

Finally, James held that consciousness is also always of an object that is perceived as being separate from itself (what is sometime referred to as the 'intentionality' of consciousness).

Intentionality:
The directedness of consciousness; consciousness is always consciousness of something.

It is perhaps fair to say that more than any other figure William James helped to propel psychology into the modern era. As Cecil Mace has suggested, James played the central role in transforming psychology from its status as a branch of philosophy with scientific pretensions into a genuinely rigorous discipline that aimed at a scientific understanding of the human mind, albeit with some philosophical fairy dust sprinkled on top.

More generally, James introduced psychology to the wider educated public. His textbook *The Principles of Psychology*, which took 12 years to write, and surveyed the history of psychology up until the time of its writing, was a runaway success. In the present day, though obviously dated, it is generally considered a classic of the discipline, even by some scholars its most important work.

Ivan Pavlov

The Russian physiologist Ivan Pavlov hit upon the phenomenon that led to the discovery of classical conditioning by accident. He was working on canine digestion when he noticed his laboratory dogs exhibiting a curious new behaviour. They would begin to salivate whenever he or his assistant entered the laboratory. It seemed they had learned to associate his presence in the laboratory with the imminent arrival of canine snacks.

Born: 1849, Ryazan, Russia
Importance: Identified conditioning, or learning behaviours via association
Died: 1936, St Petersburg, Russia

Pavlov set about testing this conjecture in a systematic fashion by means of an experiment that has since become perhaps the most famous in the history of psychology. He devised a technique for measuring the extent of a dog's salivary secretions and was able to confirm that food automatically causes a dog to salivate. In other words, he determined that it is a hard-wired fact about dogs that they salivate while eating. In this sense, food is an unconditioned stimulus (UCS) that causes the unconditioned response (UCR) of salivation in a dog.

The interesting question was whether it would be possible to get a dog to salivate by pairing a neutral stimulus – such as the ringing of a bell – with the unconditioned stimulus. Sure enough, Pavlov found that if a bell and food are paired together frequently enough, a dog will begin to salivate as soon as it hears the bell, even if the food is nowhere to be seen. In this situation, the bell functions as a conditioned stimulus (CS) causing a conditioned response (CR) in the dog.

This kind of learning is known as classical conditioning, and its discovery sparked much research that aimed at uncovering its secrets. For example, Pavlov discovered the existence of second-order conditioning, where a CS (for example, a buzzer) will in

Above: Pavlov's legacy is assured due entirely to his discovery of classical conditioning, a type of learning that relies on pairing a neutral stimulus – for example, the ringing of a bell – with an unconditioned stimulus – for example, food.

effect function as a UCS if paired with a new neutral stimulus (for example, a black square). He also demonstrated generalization, where a stimulus similar to the original CS (for example, a bell of a slightly different pitch) will also provoke a CR; and discrimination, where a stimulus of a big enough difference (for example, a bell of a very different pitch) will not provoke a CR.

The work of Ivan Pavlov was hugely influential in the first half of the twentieth century, contributing particularly to the rise of the behaviourist school, and even in the present day remains a valuable contribution to our understanding of how learning occurs.

Edward Thorndike

The studies with animals that American psychologist Edward Thorndike conducted in the last few years of the nineteenth century were likely the first laboratory experiments ever conducted in the area of animal psychology.

Born: 1874, Williamsburg, Massachusetts
Importance: Outlined a highly important theory of reinforcement
Died: 1949, Montrose, New York

Thorndike earned his MA at Harvard University in 1897 and became an instructor in psychology at Teachers College at Columbia University in 1899, where he remained for the rest of his career. His subject was animal learning and his most famous experiments involved cats and a puzzle box. The puzzle box was an open-slatted wooden container from which it was possible to escape only by solving a puzzle – for example, by opening a latch and then pulling a lever. The reward for escaping was food. His idea was to see whether, with practice, an animal would get better at escaping from the box.

The first time he placed a cat in the box, its behaviour was random and chaotic. The cat eventually escaped, but only as a matter of luck – it just happened to hit upon the right combination of behaviours to solve the puzzle. However, over time, after repeated trials, the cat's behaviour became more and more focused towards solving the puzzle, until eventually it was able to escape as soon as it was placed into the box.

Thorndike argued that his cats manifested trial and error learning. Each successful escape, together with the reward of food, functioned to stamp the correct behaviour into the mind of the animal. The cat didn't understand its situation, or experience a moment of insight, it merely became able to reproduce the behaviour that would get it out of the box.

He also maintained that a 'law of effect' was in play during this kind of learning. This holds that if a behaviour in a particular

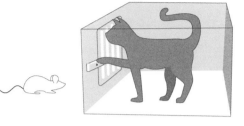

Above: Thorndike is renowned for discovering a 'law of effect', which he was able to demonstrate through his experiment of rewarding a cat with food for escaping a container by first solving a puzzle.

situation results in satisfaction, then the association between the behaviour and the situation will be strengthened. In effect, Thorndike had discovered what later came to be known as reinforcement – put simply, anything that increases the likelihood of a behaviour occurring – which became a central concept in the arsenal of behavioural psychologists.

Thorndike's reputation is largely tied up with his work on animal learning but he also made significant contributions to other areas of study, including educational psychology and psychometrics.

Law of Effect:
Behaviour that produces a favourable outcome will most likely be repeated; whereas behaviour that produces an unfavourable outcome will most likely not be repeated.

John Watson

John B. Watson's advocacy of 'behaviourism', the approach to psychology that he is largely credited with having founded, was a reaction against a prevailing orthodoxy at the turn of the twentieth century that was obsessively focused on conscious experience and that championed introspection as the means by which to uncover its fundamental elements. Watson rejected the methods of the orthodoxy as esoteric and hopelessly unscientific, noting that the typical attitude of a psychologist of this time seemed to be that if their findings were not reproduced, it was because their colleagues were just not proficient enough in the techniques of introspection.

Born: 1878, Travelers Rest, South Carolina
Importance:Pioneered the school of behaviourism
Died: 1958, New York, New York

Watson proposed that psychology should discard all references to the contents of consciousness and focus instead on observable and measurable behaviour. His aim was to propel psychology in the direction of the other natural sciences, establishing it as an objective, experimental discipline.

Watson's famous 'Little Albert' experiment, which he conducted at John Hopkins University in 1920, shows how such a science might proceed as it deals with human learning. Watson began his experiment by establishing that Albert B., an 11-month old infant, had no particular fear of a white rat. The question that interested Watson was whether it would be possible to inculcate such a fear in Albert.

To find out, he presented the rat to Albert, and then

There are...for us no instincts—we no longer need the term in psychology. Everything we have been in the habit of calling an 'instinct' today is a result largely of training.

Behaviorism

Above: Watson, the father of behaviourism, was the first to show, through his experiments with 'Little Albert', that a conditioned response can be generated in a human being.

as Albert reached out to pet it, he struck a hammer against a steel bar that was positioned just behind Albert's head. Not surprisingly, Albert reacted with fear and distress to the loud noise. It took just seven repetitions of this process before Albert started to react in fear to the mere sight of the rat. Moreover, Watson found that Albert's fear quickly generalized to other similar stimuli such as a rabbit and a fur coat.

This experiment is now notorious in the history of psychology for its problematic ethics. A particular objection is that Watson did not attempt to 'decondition' Albert's fear of the rat. Nevertheless, the 'Little Albert' experiment was the first time that a conditioned response had been demonstrated in a human, and it also showed how psychology might proceed without making reference to internal mental states.

Max Wertheimer

In 1910, Max Wertheimer was on a train travelling towards Frankfurt when he had the insight that would eventually result in the founding of the new Gestalt school of psychology. He noticed that flashing lights at a train station created the illusion of movement. The significance of this point is that it showed that perception of movement is possible even where there are no moving elements in the visual field.

Born: 1880, Prague, Kingdom of Bohemia
Importance: Foremost proponent of Gestalt theory
Died: 1943, New Rochelle, New York

Although this was already well-known, Wertheimer and his colleagues were able to show how it undermined the 'molecular' approach of the Wundtian psychologists. Perceptual experience is not built out of discrete elements, but rather structured by the whole (Gestalt) perceptual field; or as Wertheimer put it, 'There are wholes, the behaviour of which is not determined by that of their individual elements, but where the part-processes are themselves determined by the intrinsic nature of the whole'.

This point can be illustrated by considering how we tend to organize sensory information. Take the following pattern of symbols, for example: ! ! ! ? ? ! ! ! ? ? ! ! ! ? ?. We will tend to interpret it as being made up of three sets of three exclamation marks and two questions mark (rather than some alternative, but equally possible, configuration). According to Wertheimer, this is because we tend to group similar items together when interpreting sensory information.

Another principle of organization is proximity. Imagine hearing the following pattern of sound: click-click-click, pause, click-click-click, pause, click-click-click. We will tend to interpret the click sounds as belonging to three groups of three, rather than as belonging to a larger group that includes a pause, for example.

According to Wertheimer, this shows that we don't build

our perceptual experiences by attending to the discrete elements of experience, and then combining them together, but rather we interpret the elements of experience in terms of the whole context within which they appear.

Wertheimer's rejection of atomism went beyond the narrow scope of his ideas about perception and experience. He believed that science itself needed to turn away from the primitive reductionism of treating wholes as merely the sum of their parts. In the natural world, there are only rare instances where wholes are just a combination of parts. A pile of sand might count, for example. However, it is normally the case that a whole is utterly different from its constituent parts.

> There are wholes, the behaviour of which is not determined by that of their individual elements, but where the part-processes are themselves determined by the intrinsic nature of the whole.
>
> 'Gestalt Theory'

Wertheimer's son, the psychologist Michael Wertheimer, reports that his father's favourite example to illustrate this point was a soap bubble. One tiny alteration in a single bubble radically transforms the whole.

Gestalt psychology generated a vast amount of activity on the part of its proponents in its heyday in the years between the two World Wars. According to one commentator, in the twenty-five years following Wertheimer's initial experiments, 114 separate principles of organization were identified. In the present day, the insights of Gestalt psychology have largely been absorbed into the mainstream.

Edward Tolman

Like many of his contemporaries, Edward C. Tolman was attracted to behaviourism because of his dissatisfaction with orthodox introspective psychology. However, where he departed from his more radical colleagues, such as John B. Watson, was in seeing a role for cognitive factors in the learning process.

Born: 1886, West Newton, Massachusetts
Importance: Early pioneer of cognitive psychology
Died: 1959, Berkeley, California

The significance of this point can be understood by considering how a strict behaviourist would view a rat's learned ability to run a maze. The rat would be seen as merely reproducing certain muscular movements that had been 'reinforced' by the rewards that had followed its previous successful attempts to navigate the maze. The maze acts as stimulus, and the rat simply reproduces particular individual kinaesthetic responses.

Tolman rejected this view as too simplistic, and, together with his colleagues and students, conducted a series of experiments that showed some of the ways it was deficient as an explanation of learning. One of the most notable of these experiments involved a group of rats running a maze under three different conditions. Group 1 were rewarded with food each time they completed the maze, and quickly learned how to escape it; Group 2 were never rewarded for escaping the maze, and consequently spent the whole time running around randomly; Group 3 were not rewarded for the first 10 days, and during this time behaved exactly as Group 2. However, after 10 days, they were rewarded, which resulted in very rapid learning, allowing them soon to catch up with the rats in Group 1.

This suggests that the rats in Group 3 had been learning about the maze the whole time they were running it, but the learning had remained latent until rewards were introduced. On the basis of this sort of evidence, Tolman argued for the existence of cognitive

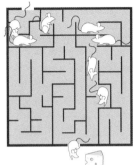

Above: Tolman's experiments demonstrated that animal learning is not merely a matter of automatic behavioural responses, but rather involves cognitive elements, including cognitive maps that function to orient an animal in space.

maps that function to orient an animal in space, thereby allowing it to produce purposive behaviour under the right circumstances. It also showed that while reinforcement might be crucial for behaviour, it isn't crucial for learning.

Tolman's importance in this history of psychology is as a pioneer of an early form of cognitive psychology at a time when the behaviourists were dominant. In showing that cognitive processes were in play during learning, his work provided an important corrective to the reductionism of strict behaviourism.

B. F. Skinner

B. F. Skinner's behaviourism is built on the simple, yet powerful, idea that if we want to explain the existence of a behaviour, then our best bet is to look at its consequences. In essence, this is just a restatement of Edward Thorndike's law of effect. However, in Skinner's hands, the scope of this idea was extended to the point where it effectively encompassed the whole of human behaviour.

Born: 1904, Susquehanna, Pennsylvania
Importance: Defined positive and negative reinforcement
Died: 1990, Cambridge, Massachusetts

Skinner's version of this idea was instantiated in his notion of operant conditioning, which refers to the shaping of behaviour by the means of rewards and punishments. This idea can be illustrated by considering how a 'Skinner box' operates. A rat is placed inside an enclosed box, within which there is a lever, which, if pressed, will immediately deliver a food pellet to the rat. At first, the rat will just run around aimlessly, but eventually it will bump into the lever with the consequence that it will be rewarded with food. This has the effect of reinforcing the behaviour that precedes the reward – that is, the lever pressing. In this way, the rat will quickly learn to go straight to the lever in order to secure the reward. Positive reinforcement, therefore, results in the emergence of lever pressing behaviour.

The strengthening of behaviour which results from reinforcement is appropriately called 'conditioning'. In operant conditioning, we 'strengthen' an operant in the sense of making a response more probable or, in actual fact, more frequent.

Science and Human Behaviour

Skinner identified other kinds of conditioning. Negative reinforcement occurs when a behaviour is strengthened because it leads to a reduction in pain. For example, he was able to train rats to press a lever by wiring it up so that it functioned to turn off a painful electric shock. Punishment can also be used to weaken certain kinds of behaviours, which presumably is the general idea that motivates the use of sanctions – including, sometimes, the infliction of pain – in order to discourage unwanted behaviours in children.

Skinner's behaviourism is undoubtedly radical in its implications. Although, unlike John Watson, he did not deny the existence of the mind, it played no part in his explanation of behaviour. As far as he was concerned, almost all behaviour is determined by patterns of positive and negative reinforcement. The power of his approach – whatever its limitations – is unquestionable. It is a striking thought that by using techniques of conditioning, Skinner was able to teach pigeons to play table tennis.

Operant conditioning: A form of learning where behaviour is modified by consequences that are either reinforcing or punishing.

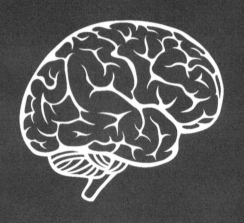

The Mind and the Person

As psychology matured in the middle part of the twentieth century, its focus shifted from behaviour to a concern with the workings and characteristics of the mind. In this section, we focus on cognitive psychology, looking at the work of luminaries such as Jerome Bruner and Noam Chomsky, and comparative psychology, through the work of psychologists such as Raymond Cattell and Hans Eysenck.

Behaviourism

A theory that denies that thoughts can regulate actions does not lend itself readily to the explanation of complex human behaviour.

Albert Bandura

Although there is no simple way to define cognitive psychology, the approach is probably best understood in terms of a metaphor drawn from computer science that sees the brain as an information processing system. The brain is not a mere passive receptacle of incoming sensory information, wedded to the task of reproducing learned responses in behaviour, but rather an active system that processes and shapes the information it receives. Cognitive psychologists tend to focus on phenomena such as perception, attention, decision-making, memory and language acquisition, being concerned to elucidate the active role played by the brain in the processes that underpin them.

Cognitive psychology emerged in the 1950s as a result of a general dissatisfaction with behaviourism, which was, particularly in North America, the dominant psychological paradigm at the time. It had become increasingly clear that in focusing exclusively on behaviour and the stimulus-response associations that supposedly underpin all learning, behaviourism was unable to account for the complexity of human thought and behaviour.

This sort of intransigent reductionism did not go unchallenged even before behaviourism came under sustained pressure from the rise of cognitive psychology. Edward Tolman's work in the 1930s, which demonstrated the importance of 'cognitive maps' for learning, and Jerome Bruner's experiments in the 1940s, which showed that perception was a dynamical phenomenon, were early examples of a departure from a strict behaviourist approach.

The beginning of the 'cognitive revolution', which within less than two decades saw cognitive psychology supplant behaviourism as the dominant psychological paradigm, is often dated to 1956, a year during which a number of events occurred that are considered pivotal to the rise of the information processing approach.

During the summer of that year, a number of academics, including John McCarthy, who coined the term 'artificial intelligence', and Marvin Minsky, convened at Dartmouth College to discuss whether machines could be made to simulate intelligence; and, later in the year, at a meeting at MIT, Noam Chomsky presented a paper that contained the ideas that would the next year become his masterpiece, *Syntactic Structures*, which sparked a revolution in our understanding of the relationship between language and cognition.

Also in 1956, Bruner et al published *A Study of Thinking*, which was the first serious investigation of the cognitive processes underlying concept formation; and George Miller published his groundbreaking paper, 'The magical number seven, plus or minus two', which described some of the limits on the human capacity to process information and is now one of the most cited papers in the history of psychology.

In the present day, cognitive psychology permeates nearly all aspects of psychological research. Although its greatest strength still lies in areas such as memory and attention, which naturally lend themselves to an information processing approach, its influence is felt in domains as diverse as cognitive therapy, cognitive development and social cognition.

Alfred Binet

Alfred Binet, a French psychologist working at the turn of the twentieth century, is renowned for developing the first genuinely useful test of intelligence, and also, more generally, for championing the cause of individual psychology, which he took to be the study of those properties of the mind that vary from individual to individual.

Born: 1857, Nice, France
Importance: Devised the first useful intelligence test
Died: 1911, Paris, France

Binet was motivated to develop his intelligence 'scale' by the thought that if it were possible to identify children who were educationally impaired, then they could be helped through the provision of special education.

His approach in this endeavour was wholly practical. He got two groups of children, one normal, the other impaired, to complete a variety of tests, and then looked for those test items that were sensitive to the difference between the two groups, and also to the difference between children and adults. In this way, together with his colleague, Theodore Simon, he was able to develop the thirty tests of increasing difficulty that comprised his original 1905 intelligence scale.

By 1908, he had revised the scale, basing it on the average performance of a normal child at a particular age. Thus, for example, at age three, a child should be able to point to their nose, eyes and mouth; at four, they should be able to repeat three digits; at eleven, name sixty words in three minutes; and at twelve, repeat seven digits. It was Binet's view that if a child was unable to complete the tasks for the age group two years behind their own, then they were part of the seven per cent of the population that would benefit from special education.

Binet was well aware of the limitations of his intelligence scale. He accepted that intelligence was a complex phenomenon

Left: Binet developed the first modern intelligence scale in 1905. By 1908, the test was revised and based on judging performance against a particular age, for instance, a three-year-old child should be able to point to their nose, eyes and mouth.

– defining it broadly as the ability to adapt to and master one's circumstances – and his test reduced intelligence to a single item only as a matter of expediency. Binet also rejected the view that intelligence was fixed, believing instead that with the right training it was possible for children to improve their level of intelligence. In the present day, Binet's intelligence scale lives on as the Stanford-Binet Intelligence Scales, which has reached its fifth iteration, and is used for clinical and neuropsychological assessment, early childhood assessment and evaluations for special education placement.

Charles Spearman

The English psychologist Charles Spearman came to psychology relatively late in life after a fifteen-year career in the British Army. However, his tardiness did not prevent him from making breakthrough advances in statistical theory, particularly through his use of factor analysis, nor from identifying a single general factor of intelligence (*g*), a concept that is still influential in the present day, one hundred years after he originally specified it.

Born: 1863, London, England
Importance: Outlined an original two-factor theory of intelligence
Died: 1945, London, England

Spearman's discovery of *g* was the result of an analysis of the patterns of correlation between various common tests of intellectual ability. To put it simply, he discovered that if somebody was good at one kind of test – for example, a test of sensory discrimination – then they also tended to be good at other, seemingly unrelated, kinds of tests (for example, tests of word recall). This suggests the existence of a single factor of intelligence underpinning performance across a range of tests.

According to Spearman, a person's performance on any individual test is a function of this single general factor and also of a factor specific to the particular test. Thus, he argued that intelligence comprises two different sorts of factors: *g*, the general factor, and *s*, a multitude of specific factors.

The general factor, which Spearman conceived as having something of the character of a flow of power, is particularly important for those mental operations most commonly associated with reason. In particular, it is dominant for the ability to perceive relations between concepts and for the ability to see how relations in one situation can be transferred to another. Not surprisingly, it is much less important when it comes to abilities that are a long way removed from the operation of reason. For example, it plays

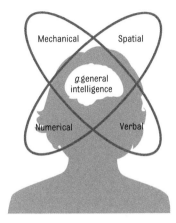

Left: Spearman identified a general factor of intelligence (*g*), which he argued underpinned the performance of individuals across a range of tests of cognitive ability.

virtually no role at all in the ability to distinguish one tone from another.

Spearman's idea of a general factor of intelligence sparked a huge amount of interest and controversy, and is very much a live topic today. Although a number of the criticisms levelled against his particular schema have stuck – in particular the possibility that there might be other general abilities in addition to *g* – the existence of something akin to his *g* has good evidential support.

Factor analysis:
A statistical technique that reduces a large number of factors to a smaller number of dimensions by looking for correlations between the original factors.

Cyril Burt

Upon his death in 1971, British psychologist Cyril Burt was eulogized as one of the discipline's 'brightest stars' – the 'dean of the world's psychologists', as one commentator put it. His achievements included a British Academy fellowship and more than 350 articles published in a sixty-year career. Six years later, his reputation lay in tatters, destroyed by mounting evidence that he had committed systematic scientific fraud.

Born: 1883, London, England
Importance: Pioneered research that seemed to prove the heritability of IQ
Died: 1971, London, England

Burt's posthumous fall from grace is a complicated story, but in essence he seems to have based his classic studies of monozygotic (identical) twins reared apart (MZAs) on fabricated data in order to bolster his claim that intelligence is largely an inherited phenomenon.

In order to understand what happened, the first thing to note is that the IQ test scores of monozygotic twins are highly correlated. This is exactly what you'd expect if intelligence is largely fixed by a person's genes, but crucially it is also what you'd expect if intelligence is a product of the environment, because twins are almost always brought up together. It is this point that makes monozygotic twins reared apart gold dust to psychologists investigating the heritability of intelligence. If the 'hereditarians' are right that intelligence has a large genetic component, then one would still expect the IQ scores of MZAs to be highly correlated.

> Tests of scholastic attainment, the tests of general knowledge, the tests of emotional and moral character must not be mixed with the tests of intelligence and other psychical capacities.
>
> 'The Measurement of Intelligence by the Binet Tests'

Above: Burt was renowned in his lifetime for his twin studies that seemingly showed that intelligence is in large part hereditary.

However, his legacy was tarnished when it came to light that he had fabricated much of his data.

This is exactly what Burt seemed to have established in three key studies of MZAs, all of which showed that pairs of identical twins reared apart had very similar IQ scores. These studies were considered to be absolutely crucial evidence.

Unfortunately, research by the psychologist Leon Kamin, conducted shortly after Burt's death, uncovered a problem with his data; namely, that it was just too good to be true. Put simply, Burt's three studies reported an identical result, despite the fact they were published many years apart, and despite the final study including three times as many twins as the first study. This is a virtual statistical impossibility, which together with a number of other anomalies, led researchers to conclude that Burt must have fabricated his data.

Not everybody agreed, but what is certain is that the results of Burt's studies cannot now be considered reliable scientific findings.

Gordon Allport

In 1924, the American psychologist Gordon Allport began to teach a course at Harvard University, titled 'Personality: Its Psychological and Social Aspects'. Nowadays, there would be nothing particularly unusual about that, but ninety years ago, Allport was a pioneer in the field of personality psychology, and his was the first such course on the American continent.

Born: 1897, Montezuma, Indiana
Importance: Important proponent of humanistic psychology
Died: 1967, Cambridge, Massachusetts

Allport distinguished between two different approaches to the study of personality. 'Nomothetic' approaches focus on the personality characteristics that individuals share in common. So, for example, where people place on a general scale of introversion/ extroversion. 'Idiographic' approaches, which Allport favoured, focus on the uniqueness of every individual and specifically on the particular traits and dispositions that they manifest.

Together with his colleague Henry Odbert, Allport identified approximately 18,000 terms that describe personal characteristics, which he reduced to 4,504 traits proper. Allport suggested a hierarchical organization for the traits that characterize any particular individual. *Cardinal* traits are so all-encompassing that, in effect, they define a person, constituting a ruling passion. Most people, however, do not have a single predominant trait in this sense. Rather, their personalities are built out of *central* traits, which, though few in number, nevertheless constitute the primary mode by which they deal with the world. So, for instance, a person might be generally optimistic, or analytical, or aggressive.

Finally, there are *secondary* traits, which are less consistent, and tend to be contingent upon particular situations. Here, we're talking about tastes, preferences and the like, which might only be known by those closest to the person.

There is a puzzle in Allport's analysis. He claimed that every individual personality is unique, yet the traits he identified seem not to be unique (we all understand what it means to be happy, for example). His way out of this puzzle was to argue that it is the particular configuration of traits that is crucial. Thus, personality in general can be seen as the 'the dynamic organization within the individual of those psychophysical systems that determine his characteristic behaviour and thoughts'.

Beyond the narrow scope of his analysis of personality, Allport hoped for a psychology that rejected the behaviourist obsession with observable behaviour, and which took proper account of the full gamut of human experience. This humanistic psychology would energize the discipline, allowing it to deal with the full range of human problems in both their subjective and objective guises.

Although Allport emphasized the importance of intuition, or experiential knowledge, he didn't think it was sufficient on its own. As Roy DeCarvalho points out, Allport believed that knowledge of human phenomena is hierarchically organized. The psychologist begins with simple, bold claims, and then moves on to careful technical work by which hypotheses are refined and confirmed (or disconfirmed). In this way, humanistic psychology aims for a science that is inclusive, featuring both subjective and objective elements. In the present day, it is as a proponent of humanistic psychology that Allport is perhaps best known.

Raymond Cattell

The British-born, American-based psychologist Raymond Cattell is renowned as much for how he conducted psychological research as he is for the discoveries that he made. He pioneered the use of multivariate analysis, which looks at the effect of multiple, interacting variables on thought and behaviour, and used complex mathematical techniques, in particular, factor-analysis, in order to draw out the significant patterns in his data.

Born: 1905, West Bromwich, England
Importance: Devised a groundbreaking trait theory of personality
Died: 1998, Honolulu, Hawaii

Cattell's mathematical leanings are strikingly illustrated in the fact that he once conceptualized personality in the form of an equation: $R = f(S, P)$.

This might look complicated but actually isn't. It simply means that a person's behavioural response (R) is a function of the situation they confront (S) and their personality (P). This lines up with his definition of personality as that which tells what a person will do when they are placed in a particular situation.

Cattell's most significant substantive contribution to the discipline of psychology is probably his trait theory of personality. He distinguished between 'surface' traits, which are clusters of behaviour that tend to be attached to a label in the ordinary language of personality, and 'source' traits, which are the underlying building blocks of personality.

Cattell's approach was thoroughly empirical. He started by looking at the 4,504 trait names identified by Gordon Allport, managing to whittle this data down to just 171 traits by discarding synonyms. He then looked at how these traits correlate together, eventually identifying 46 clusters, which constitute surface traits. He argued that these 46 surface traits make up the personality sphere – the total domain of personality traits.

Dominance

Privateness   Emotional Stability

Rule-Consciousness   Reasoning

Sensitivity   Abstractedness

Apprehension   Warmth

Vigilance   Perfectionism

Social Boldness
                                           Openness to change
Tension   Liveliness

Self-Reliance

Above: Cattell used statistical techniques in order to demonstrate that there are 16 primary personality factors, including, for example, warmth, perfectionism and emotional stability.

Cattell uncovered the source traits that constitute the structure of personality by performing factor-analysis on these 46 surface traits. This statistical technique, which reduces complex data to a small number of dimensions, allowed him to identify 16 primary factors of personality that explain the way that the surface traits tend to cluster together. These source traits include warmth, reasoning and emotional stability, and constitute the basis of his hugely influential 16 Personality Factor (16 PF) Questionnaire.

Jerome Bruner

Jerome Bruner, working in the United States in the years after the end of the Second World War, is one of the earliest pioneers of cognitive psychology, which moved the discipline's focus away from an exclusive interest in observable behaviour.

Born: 1915, New York, New York
Importance: Pioneering Cognitive Psychology
Died: 1998, Honolulu, Hawaii

In a renowned experiment, Bruner tested the hypothesis that our perception of an object would be affected by what he called 'behavioural determinants', particularly the social value of the perceived object and the individual need for the (socially valued) object. This is not as complex as it sounds. In essence, Bruner wanted to find out whether our perception of an object would be accentuated – that is, whether it would become more vivid – if the object were socially valued, and, if so, whether this would be affected by the extent to which the perceiver needed the object in question.

Bruner tested his hypothesis by getting two groups of children – one comprising children from affluent backgrounds, the other from poor backgrounds – to estimate the sizes of pennies, nickels, dimes, quarters and half-dollars, comparing each group against each other and also against a control group that had estimated the size of cardboard grey discs, identical in size to the various coins.

The results of this experiment strongly supported Bruner's hypothesis. The higher the value of the coin, the greater the extent to which its size was overestimated both compared to its actual size and to the control group's estimate of the size of the identical cardboard disc. Moreover, the estimates of the poor group deviated further from the actual size of the coin than the estimates of the rich group. This suggests that perception is not merely a matter of the nervous system responding passively and predictably to incoming sensory stimuli, but rather that it is an active process that is inextricably linked to the 'dynamical system that constitutes the person'.

Bruner also made a substantial contribution to our understanding of the process and culture of education. He argued that a child's cognitive development moves through three stages, each of which involves a way of representing the world. The enactive stage involves learning about the world through manipulating objects – for example, banging a drum and hearing its noise. The iconic stage involves using images, perhaps through drawing or imagination, to represent the situations encountered in the first stage. The final stage, the symbolic stage, takes the images developed in the second stage, and translates them into language. This is the starting point of abstract, symbolic knowledge.

His 1960 book, *The Process of Education*, a classic in the field of education studies, made the case for a 'spiral curriculum'. This is based on the apparently radical claim that 'any subject can be taught in some intellectually honest form to any child at any stage of development'. The key here is that all teaching must be appropriate to the child's stage of development. The child will return to topics and themes as they progress through their schooling, each time adding a layer of complexity. New learning builds on old learning, thereby reinforcing and solidifying the subject matter.

Cognitive psychology: An approach to psychology that focuses on internal mental processes, and treats the brain (and mind) as if it were akin to an information processing system.

Hans Eysenck

The German-born psychologist Hans Eysenck courted
controversy from almost the beginning of his career, shaking
up the establishment with his attacks on psychotherapy
and psychoanalysis, and upsetting liberal opinion with his
trenchant views on heredity, race and intelligence.
Although a polarizing character, there is no doubt
he made significant contributions to the discipline
of psychology, particularly through his work
on personality.

Born: 1916, Berlin, Germany
Importance: Identifying
Three Dimensions of
Personality
Died: 1997, London, England

Eysenck identified three major dimensions of
personality – extraversion-introversion, neuroticism-
stability and psychoticism-impulse control – each
of which is associated with characteristic personality traits. For
example, extraverts tend to be sociable, talkative and sensation-
seeking, whereas introverts are quiet, reserved and shy. People high
in neuroticism are anxious, moody and touchy, whereas people low
in neuroticism are even-tempered, relaxed and rational. Individuals
high in psychoticism are aggressive and antisocial, whereas those
low in psychoticism tend to be warm and empathetic.

Perhaps the most interesting aspect of Eysenck's approach
is the thoroughly biological explanation he gave for these
different personality dimensions. In essence, he thought
that personality is related to innate levels of brain arousal –
introverts, for example, have naturally high levels of arousal,
whereas extraverts have naturally low levels. This means that
introverts are going to reach their optimum level of arousal – the
point beyond which any increase in arousal becomes unpleasant
– sooner than extraverts. Therefore, introverts will tend to
avoid environments and situations that are over-stimulating.
Extraverts, on the other hand, struggle to reach their optimum

level of arousal, which means they will seek out situations where they can find plenty of stimulation.

Eysenck makes a similar kind of argument for the neuroticism dimension of personality. He argues that neurotics show greater activity in the brain's limbic system, which is responsible for regulating emotional states such as aggression, fear and sex. This makes neurotics more susceptible to stress responses in the face of minor setbacks than emotionally stable people, who have lower levels of activity in the limbic region.

Controversy followed Eysenck around from early in his career. He first got himself into trouble in the early 1950s for suggesting that psychotherapy had no therapeutic efficacy, a claim which provoked outrage at the time. But it was his support for Arthur Jensen's claim that systematic differences between the IQ test scores of different races could in part be explained by genetic factors that caused him most difficulty.

But there is an irony here. Eysenck, who was born in Berlin, had to flee Germany in the early 1930s because of his opposition to Nazism, and according to his daughter he had always hated their racial ideology.

In the present day, Eysenck is remembered primarily for his contribution to our understanding of personality, and in terms of his influence it has been said that he is the British equivalent of B. F. Skinner.

Psychoanalysis:
A therapeutic approach, originated by Sigmund Freud, which holds that mental disturbances such as neurosis, depression and anxiety are a function of unresolved conflicts that exist in the unconscious parts of the psyche.

Benjamin Libet

Benjamin Libet, an American neuropsychologist, is best known for a series of experiments he conducted in the 1980s that cast doubt on the idea that the decisions that people make are under their conscious control. The inspiration for these experiments was the discovery that conscious acts are preceded by the build-up of an electrical charge in the brain, a readiness potential, which raises the disconcerting possibility that decisions are merely a function of unconscious brain activity.

Born: 1916, Chicago, Illinois
Importance: Investigating Preconscious Decision-making
Died: 2007, Davis, California

To test whether this readiness potential occurs before a person even becomes aware that they're going to act, Libet wired people up to an electroencephalogram (EEG), and asked them to perform a simple task, such as a flick of a wrist, whenever they wanted to do so. They were also asked to record a clock-time associated with their first awareness that they were going to act. This gave Libet three bits of data: the time of the act, the time of the person's awareness that they were going to act and the time of the appearance of the readiness potential (which was measured using the EEG).

The conscious mental cannot exist without the brain processes that give rise to it. However, having emerged from brain activities as a unique 'property' of that physical system, the mental can exhibit phenomena not evident in the neural brain that produced it.

Mind Time

The experiment showed that the readiness potential occurs in the brain some 350 milliseconds before a person knows that they are going to act. This led Libet to the startling conclusion that the 'initiation of the freely voluntary act appears to begin in the brain unconsciously'.

Libet did not accept that this eliminated a role for the conscious will in the decision-making process. A person's awareness that they are going to act occurs some 150 milliseconds before the act itself. According to Libet, this is enough time for the conscious will to exercise a power of veto over any potential act.

Not surprisingly, Libet's work has attracted a lot of criticism, perhaps the most interesting of which focuses on the relationship between the readiness potential and the decision to act. For example, researchers such as Alfred Mele and Peter Clarke have pointed out that it's difficult to judge exactly when you become aware that you're going to act, and there is evidence that the gap between the readiness potential and this awareness disappears if you use a different method to estimate the time of the occurrence of the awareness.

However, there has been subsequent research that seems to confirm Libet's findings. In particular, fMRI studies, such as those performed by neuroscientist John-Dylan Haynes and his team, show that changes occur in the brain predictive of an upcoming decision several seconds before the decision occurs.

Libet thought that the temporal relation he found in the laboratory between unconscious brain processes and voluntary acts would hold in the more complicated decision-making situations of everyday life, but he denied that this meant we should give up on the idea of free will altogether. Instead, he argued that non-determined free will was a better scientific option than its denial by determinist theory.

Albert Bandura

Albert Bandura's social learning theory, which he first developed while working at Stanford University in the 1950s, rests on the proposition that learning occurs not only through the effects of one's own direct actions, but also by means of modelling (or imitation). Put simply, we learn by observing others. The 1961 Bobo doll experiment, one of the most famous in the history of psychology, provides strong evidence to support this contention.

Born: 1925, Mundare, Alberta, Canada
Importance: Developing Social Learning Theory

Bandura and his colleagues exposed children between the ages of three and six to an adult model – an actor – behaving violently towards a Bobo doll. They hypothesized that this group of children would manifest higher levels of aggression than a control group when allowed to play with a Bobo doll themselves later on. The results of the experiment confirmed the hypothesis; the children exposed to the violent model tended to reproduce exactly the behaviour they had witnessed.

Although the basic premise of social learning theory is straightforward, there is complexity in the detail. Bandura identified a number of factors that have to be in place for successful learning to occur. If you want to learn, then you have to attend to the behaviour being modelled. You also have to retain the information you have witnessed, which relies on it being codified, and which is facilitated by mental rehearsal. Having retained the information, you have to be able to reproduce it. And finally, you have to be motivated to reproduce the behaviour you have learned.

Motivation is key to explaining the distinction between learning and performance. Reinforcement and punishment are important motivators, even when experienced merely vicariously.

Above: Bandura, the originator of social learning theory, showed that people can learn simply by observing others. The famous 1916 Bobo doll experiment provided strong evidence to support Bandura and his theory that children exposed to violence tend to replicate that behaviour.

In a 1965 Bobo doll experiment, Bandura found that children who had witnessed the violent model being reprimanded for his behaviour were much less likely to reproduce the violent behavior themselves when playing with the doll later on. According to Bandura, this shows that while reinforcement and punishment are not necessary for learning to occur, they can be necessary for performance. Bandura's social learning theory has been hugely influential. In particular, it has been deployed in order to explore the effects of the media on aggression and antisocial behaviour.

Norman Geschwind

Norman Geschwind, an American neurologist, was fascinated by the relationship between higher cognitive functioning – in particular, language – and the underlying neurological processes that govern it. He came to this interest through his work with aphasic patients – people who are unable to formulate and/or understand language – at the Boston VA Hospital, where he was employed as a staff neurologist in the late 1950s. This set the pattern for his career, with many of his most important studies dealing with what happens when the brain goes wrong.

Born: 1926, New York, New York
Importance: Transformed our understanding of behavioural neurology
Died: 1984, Boston, Massachusetts

An early study of brain-tumour patient 'P. J. K.' is characteristic of Geschwind's general approach. The patient was a 41-year-old police officer who had been admitted to the hospital after suffering several neurological symptoms. It was discovered he had a brain tumour, which was removed surgically.

Postoperatively, as expected, the patient manifested a number of neurological deficits, including disorientation in time, memory impairment and speech errors. However, Geschwind's team noticed something unusual. The patient could write correctly using his right hand, producing normal sentences and making no spelling mistakes. But he could not write with his left hand. His attempt to write down the

We had to point out that we couldn't say that 'the patient knew what was in his left hand' and that 'the patient could speak normally', since that part of the patient which could speak normally was not the same part of the patient which 'knew what was in the left hand'.

'Disconnexion syndromes in animals and man, II'

alphabet resulted in many unrecognizable letters. On dictation, he would produce legible words, but the wrong words.

This was not simply a matter of the patient having motor difficulties with his left hand. The same thing happened if he tried to type his name or type out words given to him in dictation. The patient himself was astonished at his inability to get things right with his left hand, and would try to correct the problems, which would just result in the same thing happening again.

Other curious problems also became apparent. For example, if the patient held an object out of his own sight in his left hand, he could manipulate it in a way that suggested he understood its proper use. However, he would be completely unable to give a correct verbal description of it, or to select it from among a group of objects with his right hand, despite the fact he could later select it with his left hand and also draw it with his left hand.

> **Corpus callosum:**
> The thick bundle of nerves that connects the brain's two hemispheres.

Geschwind, and his colleague, Edith Kaplan, argued that the most likely explanation for this pattern of neurological deficit was a disconnect between the two hemispheres of the brain. P. J. K. was able to accomplish tasks that could be handled autonomously by just one hemisphere, but as soon as a task required a transfer of information between hemispheres, he floundered. Geschwind hypothesized that the cause of this phenomenon was a lesion of the corpus callosum.

Perhaps the most important general point about this sort of research is that it does more than simply help us to understand how things can go wrong in the brain. Put simply, if we understand neurological dysfunction, then we are at least part of the way to understanding how the brain works when it's functioning normally.

Donald Broadbent

The British psychologist Donald Broadbent was at the centre of the move away from behaviourism that occurred within academic psychology in the middle part of the twentieth century. In particular, his groundbreaking studies of attention, a topic that had been largely ignored for fifty years, were indicative of a burgeoning interest in the way that the mind acquires, processes and stores information.

Born: 1926, Birmingham, England
Importance: Proposed a new model of attention processing for the brain
Died: 1993, Aylesbury, England

Broadbent's major research interest was selective attention, which refers to our ability to concentrate on particular pieces of information, while filtering out all non-relevant material. Together with Colin Cherry, he developed dichotic listening as a procedure with which to study this phenomenon. This technique involves presenting a subject with two competing streams of auditory information, one sent to each ear via a pair of headphones, and then asking them to attend to just one of the streams, and to repeat it aloud as soon as they hear it – a practice termed 'shadowing'.

The proper analogy for the most speculative statements … [is] with propositions about mountains on the other side of the moon, which are perfectly meaningful but rather difficult to test.

Behaviour

Experiments conducted in the 1950s using this technique showed that we process very little of the non-shadowed information. We might be able to identify whether the speaker is male or female, but we won't be able to say what they're talking about or even whether their message has been reversed.

Broadbent proposed an early filter model of selective attention to account for this phenomenon. He argued that if the brain were able to process every input before selection, then there would be no reason for selection to occur at all. Therefore, the fact that it does occur is evidence that the brain is a 'limited capacity channel', where the utility of a selection system is that it produces an economy in mechanism. Selection occurs through the operation of a filter that uses the gross physical characteristics of an input – for example, its spatial location – to isolate it for further processing, discarding everything else. The filter passes the selected input onto the limited capacity channel, where it is processed for content and meaning.

Broadbent's model is a very early attempt to understand the brain as an information-processing system. The emergence of new evidence has cast doubt on his specific claims; however, there is no doubting the influence of his general approach, which is an early example of what is now known as cognitive psychology.

Broadbent also worked hard to raise the profile of psychology. Psychology was on the up in the United States, but it was viewed with a certain amount of suspicion in Britain. Broadbent attempted to rectify this by frequent radio and television appearances, and by writing a book, *Behaviour*, for the general public that was published in 1961.

In an assessment of his life and work, published a year after his death, Lawrence Weizkrantz attributed a paradigm shift in both academic and applied psychology to the contribution made by Broadbent. The information-processing approach had come to permeate both domains.

Limited capacity channel: The brain is a limited capacity channel in the sense that there is an upper limit on the amount of incoming information that it is able to process (which means that information has to be filtered).

Noam Chomsky

In his celebrated work of linguistic theory, *Syntactic Structures*, published in 1957, Noam Chomsky took on the then dominant behaviourist theory of language acquisition, which held that children develop language as a result of training and experience, arguing instead that humans are born with an innate ability to understand the principles that underpin the structure of language.

Born: 1928, Philadelphia, Pennsylvania
Importance: Transformed the field of modern linguistics

In its detail, Chomsky's theory is dauntingly complex; however, it is possible to get a general sense of how it works. The first point to understand is that language operates at two different levels. Consider, for example, the following phrases: 'The cat hissed at the mouse'; and 'The mouse was hissed at by the cat'. These phrases have a different surface structure, but at the level of their deep structure – the level of meaning – they are identical.

Chomsky argues that humans have an inborn ability to move easily between these two levels of language. We are able to construct novel, but meaningful, sentences, because we are able to transform deep structure (the level of meaning) into surface structure (the level of particular utterances). The precise mechanism of this transformation relies on a 'transformational grammar' that allows people to convert the meaning of what they want to say into particular words and phrases. Put simply, our linguistic ability is built on the set of innate, universal, abstract rules that make it possible for us to move back and forth between the surface and deep structures of language – that is, between the level of specific utterances and the level of meaning.

The evidence for something like Chomsky's view is persuasive, not least because the alternative conception, that language acquisition proceeds by means of the selective reinforcement of

Above: Whilst words and their meanings must be learned, Chomsky argued that our linguistic ability is rooted in an innate ability to transform the deep structure of language, the level of meaning, into particular words and phrases.

correct linguistic performance, is unconvincing given that the number of sentences to which children are ever exposed is but a tiny fraction of the number they are able to generate.

Chomsky's ideas about transformational grammar, though perhaps not in their detail a majority view, revolutionized linguistics in the second half of the twentieth century. Although in the present day Chomsky is better known for his social commentary, there is no doubt that it is for his contributions to linguistic theory that he will be remembered.

George Sperling

George Sperling, an American cognitive psychologist, came to prominence in the early 1960s as a result of a study that demonstrated the existence of what is now called 'iconic memory' – a fast-decaying store of visual information.

Born: 1934, New York, New York
Importance: Proved we see a brief, perfect vision of the world that quickly decays

Sperling's groundbreaking study set out to answer the question, 'How much can be seen in a single brief exposure?' By 'brief', he meant very brief – imagine, for example, a lightning flash illuminating a scene that you are required to describe. The interest of the question lay partly in the fact that, when asked to report what they had seen during such a brief exposure, people claim to have seen more than they are able to report. This raises the possibility that we have information very briefly available to us that we're not able to report on because it decays too quickly.

Sperling explored this possibility by means of a cleverly constructed experiment that he conducted in 1960. He exposed people to a grid comprising three rows of three letters for a mere 20 milliseconds, and then asked them to recall the letters. On average, his subjects were able to recall about half of the letters, which was in line with the findings of previous research. However, his innovation was to run the experiment again, this time adding in an audible tone, which signalled which row the subject had to recall. The results improved dramatically, with few mistakes being made, which showed that all nine letters are available for recall, but only for a very brief period of time.

An interesting question here is: 'just how brief is the duration of our iconic memory?' Sperling tested this by delaying the tone that signalled which row had to be recalled. He found that with a delay, accuracy of recall drops off very quickly. If the tone is delayed by as little as one second, then performance is no better than when the subjects are asked to recall the whole grid.

The results of this experiment led Sperling to develop one of the earliest information-processing models of visual perception, which stressed the importance of iconic memory, or what Sperling termed "visual information storage" as the first stage in the processing of visual information. The model had three basic parts. (1) The observer sees the stimulus image for a brief period. (2) They scan the stimulus, recognizing and selecting certain information to rehearse. (3) The observer is then able to report back on what they remember of the rehearsal.

Sperling's work retains its influence. Most models of visual perception include a place for an initial iconic store that functions as the crucial first step in the processing of visual information.

In the years since his discovery of iconic memory, Sperling has continued to work within the domain of physiological psychology, motivated by a desire to 'apply the quantitative and theoretical methods of the hard sciences to the analysis of cognitive processes'. In particular, he has developed a number of mathematical models that can be applied to various facets of perception and attention.

> **Iconic memory:**
> A fast-decaying store of visual information that is accessible for processing, but only for a very brief period of time.

Michael Gazzaniga

Michael Gazzaniga's pioneering work with split-brain patients in the 1960s and 1970s led him to the radical view that, if conscious unity is disrupted by a fissure between the brain's two hemispheres, you'll get a situation where two minds coexist within the same brain as 'two completely conscious entities, in the same manner as conjoined twins are two completely separate persons'.

> Born: 1939, Los Angeles, California
> Importance: Dramatically advanced our insights into the brain's hemispheres

The split-brain procedure, which involves severing a patient's corpus callosum (the band of fibres connecting the brain's two hemispheres), has been performed only rarely, as a treatment for intractable epilepsy. The consequence of the procedure is that the two hemispheres are no longer able to communicate with each other, which provides psychologists with the opportunity to study whether the hemispheres specialize for particular tasks.

The standard experimental technique developed by Gazzaniga (and others, such as Roger Sperry), involves presenting a visual stimulus exclusively to one or the other hemisphere, and then getting the subject to answer questions and/or complete tasks. A striking result of this research is the extent to which the right-hemisphere is deficient in its ability to produce and understand language. For example, if you flash an image to the right-hemisphere, almost inevitably a split-brain subject will say they haven't seen an object (because language is dominant in the left-hemisphere). However, if you then instruct them to retrieve the object using their left hand (which is controlled by the right-hemisphere), they will have no problem in doing so.

The idea that the right-hemisphere has its own distinct mental life, which it is unable to express, is supported by work done with a young patient known as Paul S., who is unique among split-brain

Left: Gazzaniga's work demonstrated that the two hemispheres of the brain are capable of operating as distinct, independent entities, each with its own set of priorities, values and functions.

subjects in possessing some right-hemisphere language ability. This enabled Gazzaniga and his colleagues to interrogate each of Paul's hemispheres separately. The results were stunning. The two hemispheres appeared to have their own value systems and priorities. Perhaps most striking was the response that each hemisphere gave to a question about a future career. The left-hemisphere indicated that it wanted to become a draughtsman, a response that coincided with Paul's earlier expressed wish. But the right hemisphere had a different idea: when instructed to spell out its ideal job, it responded 'automobile racer'.

Split-brain patients:
Patients who have had their corpus callosum severed, thereby making it impossible for information to pass between the two brain hemispheres.

Antonio Damasio

The Portuguese-born neuroscientist Antonio Damasio has spent a large part of his career exploring the relationship between brain, emotion and rationality. In particular, he is noted for developing a 'somatic marker hypothesis', which holds that emotion, and its biological substrate, underpin the ability of humans to make rational decisions.

> **Born:** 1944, Lisbon, Portugal
> **Importance:** Argued that emotion enables us to make rational decisions.

The most compelling evidence to support this hypothesis comes from Damasio's work with brain-damaged patients. The case of 'Elliot', which Damasio discusses in his 1994 book, *Descartes' Error*, is particularly striking.

Elliot's problems began after an operation to remove a brain tumour resulted in damage to his ventromedial prefrontal cortex. Prior to the surgery, Elliot had been a successful businessman, but afterwards, his life rapidly began to unravel because he could no longer make even simple decisions. He was unable to dress himself in the morning because he couldn't decide what to wear, it took him 30 minutes to make a simple appointment, and choosing a place to eat lunch could take him until supper time.

> I continue to be fascinated by the fact that feelings are not just the shady side of reason but that they help us to reach decisions as well.
>
> 'Feeling Our Emotions'

Curiously, Elliot did not manifest any of the standard cognitive deficits. Damasio reports that he was highly intelligent, articulate and had a good understanding of social conventions and morality. However, Damasio had noticed that Elliot seemed emotionally flat – in particular, he did not appear to be upset about his predicament.

Damasio argues that emotion is necessary for decision making, because it functions to provide cues that enable people to narrow down the vast range of choices that confront them whenever they make even a simple decision. Thus, for example, Elliot did not instantly know that it would be a good idea to get dressed in the morning, because he had no sense of the embarrassment that would inevitably follow if he didn't make that choice.

Damasio and his colleagues produced some interesting experimental evidence supporting the proposition that emotion is necessary for decision-making using what is known as the Iowa Gambling Test. In this test, participants are asked to choose cards from four decks. Good cards bring monetary reward, bad cards, monetary loss. Some decks contain more good cards than bad cards. Other decks more bad cards than good cards.

In normal circumstances, people doing the test will soon learn which decks are good decks, and draw cards exclusively from those decks. However, Damasio's patients did not do this – they carried on drawing cards from both decks.

Damasio measured the stress reactions of the participants. His patients, because of ventromedial prefrontal cortex damage, did not experience stress in the normal way. Their stress response to a bad result – i.e., drawing a card associated with a monetary loss – was suppressed. This hampered their decision-making, because they were unable to incorporate a fear of punishment into their decision-making calculus.

Damasio's view that emotion is central to the decision-making process is no longer particularly unusual among neuroscientists and psychologists. However, it remains a marginal view in wider mainstream culture, where emotion is normally seen as the antithesis of reason.

Elizabeth Loftus

The American cognitive psychologist Elizabeth Loftus is generally considered one of the most influential living psychologists. Her research focuses primarily on the ways that memory can fail, and it has been important in shaping how we understand phenomena such as eyewitness testimony and false memory syndrome.

Born: 1944, Los Angeles, California
Importance: Transformed cognitive psychology with her research on memory

Loftus is the architect of many classic studies, one of the earliest of which features two experiments she conducted with John Palmer that looked at how accurately we remember the details of a complex event such as a traffic accident.

In the first experiment, subjects were shown a number of video recordings depicting a traffic accident, and then asked a series of questions about the events that unfolded. The key question varied in a crucial way. Half the subjects were asked how fast the cars were going when they hit each other; the other half had different words substituted in for 'hit' – smashed, collided, bumped and contacted. The idea was to see whether the language used affected the estimate of speed, and the results clearly showed that it did – for example, the mean estimate for 'smashed' was 40.5 mph compared to only 31.8 for 'collided'.

The second experiment explored the more focused question of whether language affects memory. The procedure

> How is it possible for people to acquire elaborate and confident false memories? A growing number of investigations demonstrate that under the right circumstances false memories can be instilled rather easily in some people.
>
> 'Creating False Memories'

was the same as before, except this time the subjects returned after a week, and answered some follow-up questions about the accident. The key question was, 'Did you see any broken glass?' There was no broken glass depicted in the accident, but Loftus predicted that those subjects who had previously been asked the 'smashed' question would report having seen glass more often than those who had been asked the 'hit' question.

Again, this is precisely what the results showed, leading Loftus to conclude that by using the word 'smash', the experimenter attached a label to the accident, which had the consequence of causing 'a shift in the memory representation of the accident in the direction of being more similar to a representation suggested by the verbal label'.

The fact that memories can be affected by external information supplied after the fact is clearly of huge significance if one has to make judgements about the accuracy of a person's recall. It is this sort of real-world consequence that makes Loftus's work among the most significant psychological research conducted in the last 50 years.

From Birth to Death

Developmental psychology
emerged as a distinct discipline in
the 1930s and 1940s. It focuses
on the behavioural and cognitive
changes that occur in individuals
as they move from birth through to
death. In this section, we examine
the developmental theories of Jean
Piaget, Lawrence Kohlberg and
Erik Erikson, and also look at how
the psychologists John Bowlby and
Mary Ainsworth treated the issue of
attachment in young infants.

All in the Genes?

It is in the most unqualified manner that I object to
pretensions of natural equality. The experiences of the
nursery, the school, the University... are a chain of proofs to
the contrary.

Francis Galton

The debate concerning the impact of nature versus nurture (or
heredity versus environment) on human thought and behaviour is
one of the most contentious in the whole of psychology. This is not
surprising, because there's a lot at stake. If, for example, it turns
out that intelligence is largely an inherited trait, then it raises the
possibility that social inequality is written in the genes, and that no
amount of education will compensate for a deficit in natural ability.

It is easy enough to identify psychologists who are at the
extreme ends of this dispute. Arnold Gessell, for example, one
of the earliest pioneers of developmental psychology – which
looks at how the maturation process affects thought and
behaviour – was committed to a thoroughly biological theory
of development. Influenced by the ideas of Charles Darwin, he
emphasized the intractable impact of genes on the developmental
process, denying that parents or teachers could do much to alter
its progress.

Gessell believed that the developmental path of an individual,
both physical and psychological, is set down before birth.
An individual's behaviour patterns, personality and mental
capabilities are inherited traits in just the same way as their
patterns of physical growth. He did not deny that culture had
an impact, but argued that an individual's genetic make-up will
determine 'how, what, and to some extent even when' they learn.

Contrast this view with the extreme environmentalism of John B. Watson's behaviourist account of learning. He famously claimed that if he were given a dozen healthy infants, and his own specialized world to bring them up in, he could guarantee 'to take any one at random and train him to become any type of specialist I might select – a doctor, lawyer, artist, merchant-chief and yes, even beggar-man and thief, regardless of his talents, penchants, abilities, vocations and race of his ancestors'. According to this view, heredity is irrelevant, and learning is just a matter of conditioning the right stimulus-response connections.

We now know that neither of these views is correct. In fact, with particular individuals, it isn't possible to separate out the genetic and environmental aspects of their development. The complexities here are clear in Piaget's famous theory of cognitive development.

Piaget maintained, as we'll see later in this chapter, that humans possess a genetically determined timetable that governs the emergence of particular cognitive abilities. However, the process of development itself is the function of a complex interaction between biological maturation and environmental experience. Put simply, biology provides the apparatus that enables the process of cognitive development, but development only occurs as the individual encounters an environment that poses challenges that need to be solved. Thus, Piaget argued, intelligence consists in a 'set of structures constructed by continuous interaction between the subject and the external world'.

The issue of nature versus nurture is by no means settled. Although progress has been made in the sense that, in the present day, neither extreme hereditarianism nor extreme environmentalism is seen as a realistic option, the debate about the precise role played by genes and the environment still rumbles on.

Jean Piaget

There is no doubt that the Swiss psychologist Jean Piaget is one of the discipline's standout figures. He is renowned for his work on cognitive development, and particularly for the idea that human intellectual abilities develop according to a genetically determined timetable. It was Piaget's view that children and adults understand and interact with their environment in qualitatively different ways.

Born: 1896, Neuchâtel, Switzerland
Importance: Recognized as a pioneer in cognitive development studies
Died: 1980, Geneva, Switzerland

Piaget identified four separate stages of development. The sensorimotor stage (0–2 years) is characterized by the achievement of object permanence, which is the awareness that objects have their own separate and independent existence. This is followed by the preoperational stage (2–7 years), during which the child develops the ability to use and manipulate symbols, including language. At this point, the ability to generalize beyond what is immediately given in experience has not yet developed and the child cannot yet apply logical principles. These abilities begin to emerge during the third, concrete operational stage (7–11 years), during which the child also becomes less egocentric in orientation, in part because they gain an awareness that their viewpoint is only one among many. The final, formal operational stage, which normally starts between the ages of 11 and 15, is characterized by the ability to engage in decontextualized, abstract thought. According to Piaget, almost everybody will achieve this stage of development by the time they are 20 years old.

Piaget argued that intellectual development is driven specifically by a process of assimilation, disequilibrium and accommodation. The idea here is that a child makes use of behavioural and mental schemas in order to make sense of the world. If a child comes across some genuinely new phenomenon,

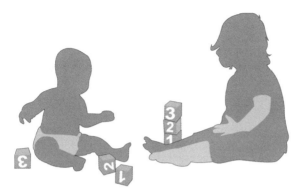

Above: Piaget's theory of development holds that human cognitive maturation occurs in distinct stages, and is governed by a genetically determined timetable. During the first stage the child develops an awareness that objects have their own separate and independent existence. During the second, the child is able to manipulate symbols, including language and numerals.

then they will not be able to assimilate the experience to the existing schema. This results in a state of disequilibrium. The way through this roadblock is to change the existing schema in order to accommodate the new experience, thereby re-establishing a state of equilibrium. It is by this general process of adaptation that intellectual progress occurs. The fact that so many outstanding psychologists, including Vygotsky and Kohlberg, have been influenced by Piaget's ideas is indicative of the extent of his importance to the discipline.

Lev Vygotsky

The ideas of the Soviet psychologist Lev Vygotsky did not make an immediate impact in the West, partly because he wrote in his native Russian language, and partly because his works were suppressed by the Soviet authorities during the middle part of the twentieth century. It was only in the early 1960s, with the publication of his book, *Thought and Language*, that his work came to wider attention, which makes it remarkable that in the present day, he is second only to Piaget in importance as a developmental psychologist.

Born: 1896, Orsha, Russia
Importance: Investigated the cultural and social nature of cognitive development
Died: 1934, Moscow, Russia

Although Vygotsky's work is fragmented and incomplete – a consequence of his premature death at the age of 37 – it is possible to identify a number of key themes and ideas. Perhaps the most important is the claim that cognitive development is thoroughly social and cultural in nature. In particular, Vygotsky believed that the higher mental functions, such as reasoning and language, emerge out of concrete social experience.

The fact that Vygotsky lived and worked in the Soviet Union is relevant here. In the Western tradition, individualism rules the day, cognitive development is something that occurs because of processes that are internal to the individual. However, Marxist theory insists on the socio-historical nature of consciousness, zooming in on the way in which our actions and thinking are moulded by concrete historical forces.

This results in an apparently paradoxical shift in the focus of attention. If you want to study consciousness or cognitive development, then you've got to start with factors that exist outside the individual human mind. The claim here isn't that consciousness can be reduced to social reality, mirroring its form in an objective way. Rather, consciousness emerges in a dialectical (interactive) relationship with the socio-historical world. As two

Marxist psychologists put it, 'man's consciousness is formed not by material production but by the personal relationships and by the products of cultural development of society'.

In Vygotsky's work, the concept of the 'zone of proximal development' (ZPD) is perhaps his most important attempt to conceptualize the socio-historical origins of mental functioning. He defined this as 'the distance between the actual development level as determined by independent problem-solving and the level of potential development as determined through problem-solving under adult guidance'. This is not as complicated as it sounds. In essence, the ZPD comprises those skills that exist just beyond a child's cognitive ability, but which they are able to master with the help of a more knowledgeable other, such as a parent or teacher. In this sense, development follows learning: with the right guidance, a child can learn skills that are in advance of their current stage of development.

Developmental psychology:
The domain of psychology that looks at the changes in thought and behaviour that occur over the lifespan of an individual.

The process of learning is social not only because it occurs within the context of a social exchange, but also because the mechanisms employed to aid learning are thoroughly embedded within the history of a culture. Thus, for example, Vygotsky noted that we make use of a variety of cultural tools in order to develop our intellectual abilities, the most important of which is language. Vygotsky's ideas are frequently contrasted with those of Jean Piaget. Although both agreed that development occurs as a result of a child's active engagement with the environment, Vygotsky allowed a much greater role for directed learning and the influence of cultural factors.

Erik Erikson

The German-born, American psychologist Erik Erikson is best known for his stage theory of development, which holds that over the course of a lifetime, human beings will pass through eight psychosocial stages, each of which involves a struggle between two opposing outcomes, one adaptive, the other maladaptive.

Born: 1902, Frankfurt, Germany
Importance: Known for his stage theory of development
Died: 1994, Harwich, Massachusetts

The eight psychosocial stages are: trust versus mistrust (0–1 years); autonomy versus shame and doubt (1–3 years); initiative versus guilt (3–6 years); industry versus inferiority (6–11 years); identity versus confusion (12–18 years); intimacy versus isolation (18–35 years); generativity versus stagnation (35–64 years); and integrity versus despair (65+ years).

It is possible to get a sense of how Erikson's theory works by looking at the 'identity versus confusion' stage, which occurs during the years of adolescence. According to Erikson, the most important challenge of adolescence is to develop a strong sense of personal identity. This involves creating a robust, integrated sense of self, which is normally achieved by developing a clear idea of a future occupation or role in life.

However, the possibility of an identity crisis (a term that Erikson is credited with originating) looms large during adolescence, because the identities forged in childhood no longer suffice as the individual transitions into adulthood. A failure to develop a new identity results in role confusion, which is associated with a number of maladaptive patterns of behaviour.

Perhaps most dramatically, role confusion can lead the adolescent to adopt a negative identity, which is marked by abnormal and delinquent behaviour. This is an extreme response, but it emerges because even a negative identity is preferable to the

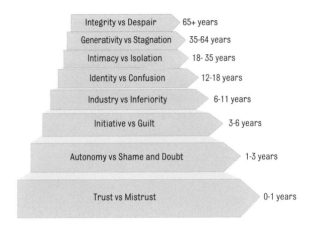

Integrity vs Despair	65+ years
Generativity vs Stagnation	35-64 years
Intimacy vs Isolation	18- 35 years
Identity vs Confusion	12-18 years
Industry vs Inferiority	6-11 years
Initiative vs Guilt	3-6 years
Autonomy vs Shame and Doubt	1-3 years
Trust vs Mistrust	0-1 years

Above: Erikson's theory of development states that there are eight distinct psychosocial stages that a human will experience over a course of a lifetime.

Each stage is characterized by a tension between two opposing outcomes, one adaptive, the other maladaptive.

alienation and estrangement that results if the adolescent is unable to achieve any coherent sense of identity.

Erikson did not believe that an individual has to meet the demands of each stage before moving on to the next stage of development. However, he argued that failure to achieve a particular adaptive outcome can result in lasting problems. For example, the toddler who fails to learn appropriate levels of trust and autonomy during the first two psychosocial stages might well have trust issues as they move into adulthood.

Erikson's idea that each stage of development requires the resolution of a crisis has proved influential and generated voluminous research, particularly in the area of adolescence studies.

John Bowlby

The English psychologist John Bowlby spent the large part of his career studying mothers and their infant children. The result of this work was a theory of attachment that changed the way psychologists think about the mother-child relation, and which threw into sharp relief the harm that can result if the bond between mother and child is disrupted by separation.

Born: 1907, London, England
Importance: Changed the way the mother-child relation is understood
Died: 1990, Skye, Scotland

Bowlby's theory of attachment is based on the idea that humans are genetically programmed to behave towards their primary caregivers in a way that is likely to secure their own survival. Put simply, evolution has rewarded those behaviours that were successful in keeping the infant close to its caregiver, because those infants were more likely to survive to pass their genes on to future generations.

Bowlby argued that the child is predisposed to form an attachment to just one particular adult – normally, their mother – a tendency he called monotropy. This is achieved most readily in a critical period that begins at about three months after birth and lasts for approximately two years. After this time, if attachment hasn't been achieved, then mothering is next to useless. The consequences of a failure in the attachment process can be profound, resulting in, for example, anxiety, aggression and delinquency.

> John Bowlby [...] revolutionized our thinking about a child's tie to the mother and its disruption through separation, deprivation, and bereavement.
>
> Inge Bretherton,
> *Developmental Psychology*

Evidence in support of Bowlby's claim that a warm, intimate and continuous relationship

Left: Bowlby argued that an extended period of separation between a mother and her child during the first years of its life could have dramatic and irreversible consequences for the child's mental well-being.

with a primary caregiver is necessary for good mental health and emotional stability is to be found in his 1944 study of 44 thieves. More than half of the young offenders in this study had been apart from their mothers for more than six months during their first five years, compared to only two out of 44 youths in a non-delinquent control group. Moreover, of the 14 youths Bowlby identified as manifesting 'affectionless psychopathy', a condition characterized by an inability to feel affection and empathy, 12 had spent significant time apart from their mothers as young children.

It was on the basis of this and other evidence that Bowlby famously declared that 'a mother's love in infancy is just as important for a child's mental health, as vitamins and minerals are for physical health'.

Mary Ainsworth

The American-Canadian psychologist Mary Ainsworth is renowned as John Bowlby's major collaborator in the development of attachment theory, and as the architect of the Strange Situation, a procedure devised towards the end of the 1960s that is used to elucidate the different forms of attachment that exist between infant and caregiver.

Born: 1913, Glendale, Ohio
Importance: Transformed child attachment studies
Died: 1999, Charlottesville, Virginia

Ainsworth's interest in patterns of attachment developed while she was working in Uganda in the 1950s. Her working hypothesis was that healthy attachment is a function of the ability of parents to respond sensitively to their child's needs and desires. Based on a nine-month longitudinal study she argued that attachment develops through stages. The infant does not initially show any preference for their mother, but by six months a strong bond will normally have been established.

This bond is manifest in characteristic behaviours on the part of the child, including infants seeking out their mothers (or main caregiver) when upset and using the mother as a secure base for exploring the wider world.

Ainsworth became interested in the small proportion of infants who showed no attachment or who could not be comforted by their mothers. This led her to devise an experimental setup termed the Strange Situation, which allowed her to explore infant attachment and exploratory behavior in situations of varying levels of stress and distress. The basic set-up involves a mother, an infant and a stranger together in a room with toys. This situation is then manipulated to see how the infant reacts to various kinds of stress. It includes two separation episodes – one where the mother leaves her infant alone with the stranger and one where the infant is left entirely alone; and two reunion episodes, where the mother returns to comfort and settle the infant.

On the basis of the range of behaviours displayed by infants during the Strange Situation, Ainsworth identified three types of attachment. Securely attached infants (70% of all infants) are distressed by the mother's absence, but will explore and play happily if the mother is present. The stranger can provide some comfort, but is not a substitute for the mother. Anxious-avoidant infants (15%) are indifferent towards the mother, and will play happily so long as an adult is present. The stranger is just as able to provide comfort as the mother. Anxious-resistant infants (15%) have an ambivalent attitude towards the mother. They are reluctant to play and explore even while the mother is present, and they are very distressed when the mother leaves. However, although they seek out contact with the mother when she returns, they appear angry and resistant when contact actually occurs. Anxious-resistant infants resist all attempts at interaction by the stranger.

> It is the insecure child who clings to his mother and refuses to leave her.
>
> *Infancy in Uganda*

It would be hard to overstate the impact of the Strange Situation procedure on the way that early child attachment has been studied. More than 40 years after it was first devised, it is still being modified, criticized and discussed. More generally, the importance of Ainsworth's research is that it provides persuasive evidence for the broader claims of Bowlby's attachment theory.

Lawrence Kohlberg

The American psychologist Lawrence Kohlberg is best known for his stage theory of moral development, which holds that at different stages of intellectual maturity, people will offer different reasons and justifications for the moral judgements they make. To demonstrate this point, Kohlberg developed a number of moral scenarios, including his famous Heinz dilemma.

Born: 1927, Bronxville, New York
Importance: Linked maturity to varying justifications for moral judgments
Died: 1987, Winthrop, Massachusetts

A woman is dying and there is one drug that might save her on sale in a single shop for $10,000. The woman's husband, Heinz, tries to borrow the money, but only manages to secure about half the drug's cost. He goes to the shopkeeper, tells him that his wife is dying and begs him to sell the drug for less, or to let him pay the balance at a later date. The shopkeeper refuses. The husband is desperate and breaks into the shop to steal the drug.

The important point about this kind of scenario is not the judgement that is reached, but rather the reasoning process that leads to the judgement.

Kohlberg identified three levels of moral development, each made up of two stages. At the pre-conventional level, notions of right and wrong are determined by authority and the possibility of punishment; and then, at the second stage of this level, by whether an action will likely result in a reward. So, for example, a young child might think Heinz behaved badly because he will probably be caught and punished.

At the conventional level, which most people reach during adolescence, moral reasoning is closely linked to social group membership. At the first stage of this level, a good action is thought to be one that will secure the approval of others; at the second stage, one that is lawful and dutiful.

According to Kohlberg, the third level of moral development, the post-conventional level, is only attained by approximately one-fifth of the population, and is much more abstract in form. For example, moral reasoning at the second stage of this level – the level of universal ethical principle orientation – will invoke universal notions such as justice, the sanctity of life and human dignity.

Kohlberg's work has particular significance for educational practice. His theory holds that moral development occurs through a fixed sequence of stages, with each stage more sophisticated in moral terms than the preceding stage. This progression can be fostered in a suitable educational environment. Thus, Kohlberg believed that cognitive and moral development is the central aim of education.

Based on a survey of empirical studies and critical reviews, Icelandic psychologist Andri Isaksson agrees that Kohlberg's ideas can play a useful role in moral education. However, several conditions must be fulfilled. Teachers need to know the developmental stage of individual students and have some knowledge of cognitive psychology. The classroom atmosphere must be accepting. Students must be exposed to the next stage of development above their own. And role-playing must assume a central role.

In a retrospective evaluation of his life and work, Harvard University psychologist, Robert Kegan, noted that the work of three senior members of Harvard's faculty had a direct line to Kohlberg, and that there was no other person, living or dead, about whom that could be said.

The Social Animal

Social psychology, which exploded
on to the psychological stage in
the years immediately following
the Second World War, looks at
how the thoughts and behaviour
of individuals are affected by the
presence of other people. In this
section, through the work and ideas
of psychologists such as Stanley
Milgram and Philip Zimbardo,
we look at a number of socially
mediated behaviours, including
obedience, conformity, scapegoating
and intergroup conflict.

Social Psychology

> ...it is not so much the kind of person a man is as the kind of situation in which he finds himself that determines how he will act.

> Stanley Milgram

The evolutionary psychologist Steven Pinker has noted that murder, rape, grievous bodily harm and theft are universal and, thus, found in all human societies. This view contrasts strongly with the philosopher Jean-Jacques Rousseau's 'noble savage' concept, which holds that humans are naturally solitary and peaceable. In light of the catastrophic history of the middle part of the twentieth century, it is tempting to dismiss the noble savage idea. However, evidence from the domain of social psychology, which accumulated in the aftermath of the horrors of the extermination camps, suggests a more nuanced, though hardly optimistic, picture.

Social psychology is the branch of the discipline that is concerned with the way our thoughts and behaviours are influenced by other people and by the social context in which we live. Elliot Aronson, one of the world's foremost social psychologists, identifies an 1898 experiment conducted by Norman Triplett that examined how performance is affected by competition as the first social psychological study. Under the rubric of social psychology, psychologists explore phenomena such as conformity, persuasion, obedience, aggression and prejudice. The evidence from social psychology is not particularly encouraging about the state of humanity. As we'll see in this chapter, Stanley Milgram's experiments showed that, under certain conditions, nearly two-thirds of us are willing to torture another human being; Henri Tajfel's research demonstrated that we are willing to discriminate against the members of an out-group even if it is at the expense of our own social group; and Philip Zimbardo's Stanford Prison Experiment showed that, given the presence of certain institutional pressures, we are predisposed to engage in hostile and abusive behaviour.

There is some ground for optimism in evidence provided by other studies. For example, Muzafer Sherif's work on intergroup conflict demonstrated that intergroup hostility will decrease, and in some circumstances disappear completely, if two disparate groups are required to work together to achieve a shared goal; and Solomon Asch's studies of conformity showed that even under significant pressure to conform, most people, most of the time, do not conform (albeit most people do conform some of the time).

Aronson points out it is wrong to draw the conclusion that people are irremediably terrible because they can be brought to do terrible things. Part of the promise of social psychology is that it will shed light on the sorts of circumstances associated with bad outcomes. As Aronson puts it, we know that some situational variables cause a large majority of 'normal' adults to behave badly. Therefore, it is of 'paramount importance that we attempt to understand the variables and the processes producing unpleasant or destructive behaviour'.

Muzafer Sherif

The Turkish-born, American-based psychologist Muzafer Sherif is properly regarded as one of the founders of social psychology. He is best known for developing realistic conflict theory, which accounts for the conflict between social groups, and for the prejudice and discrimination that results, in terms of competition for valued goods and resources. His famous Robbers Cave Experiment is taken to provide strong support for the efficacy of this theory.

Born: 1906, Ödemis, Turkey
Importance: Pioneer of social psychology and realistic conflict theory
Died: 1988, Fairbanks, Alaska

Sherif and his colleagues started the experiment, which took place in 1954 at a summer camp in Oklahoma, by dividing 22 boys – all middle-class, socially well-adjusted and of above average intelligence – into two groups, which were then kept apart to allow separate group identities to emerge. The two groups, whose members began to refer to themselves as the Rattlers and Eagles, very quickly developed group norms, hierarchies and an esprit de corps.

Sherif's hypothesis was that if two groups have conflicting aims, their members will become hostile to each other even if the groups are composed of normal, well-adjusted individuals. To test this, the Rattlers and Eagles were introduced, and told they were going to compete against each other in a series of organized games after which one group would be declared the overall winner. The relations between the two groups very rapidly deteriorated once the games began. The Rattlers and the Eagles burned each other's flags, fought, exchanged insults, sent raiding parties to each other's living quarters and stole from one another.

Rapidly escalating intergroup friction was the clear result of repeatedly bringing the two groups together in competitive and reciprocally frustrating situations. The negative attitudes that each in-group developed towards the out-group resulted

Above: Sherif's famous Robbers Cave Experiment, in which two teams took part in explicitly competitive, organized games, provides strong empirical support for his 'realistic conflict theory,' which holds that the conflict between social groups is linked to their conflicting aims and competition for valued goods and resources.

in unfavourable stereotypes, which in turn led to name-calling, derogation of the out-group and the explicit desire to avoid interacting with the out-group. The Robbers Cave Experiment thus provides strong evidence for the proposition that antagonism between social groups is linked to conflicts of interest in relation to valued goods and resources. Sherif also did groundbreaking work on communication, the self, social judgement and attitude formation and change. At his death, he was generally considered to be one of social psychology's most significant figures.

Solomon Asch

Solomon Asch was one of the twentieth century's great social psychologists. Influenced by the ideas of Gestalt psychology, he conducted important research on spatial orientation, impression formation and prestige suggestion. He also wrote what was for a long time the discipline's standout textbook, called *Social Psychology* (1952). However, it is for his groundbreaking studies of conformity that he is probably most celebrated.

Born: 1907, Warsaw, Poland
Importance: Carried out celebrated studies of conformity
Died: 1996, Haverford, Pennsylvania

It was Asch's view that the best measure of conformity is whether a person will agree with other members of a group, who all give the incorrect answer to a question that has an obvious solution. With this in mind, he devised an experimental procedure, now known as the Asch paradigm, to measure the extent of conformity.

An experimental subject is seated with six other people, all of whom are confederates of the experimenter. The experimenter presents two cards to the group, one of which has a single vertical line on it, and the other, a comparison card, three vertical lines labelled A, B and C. Each person in the group is then asked to say out loud the letter of the comparison line that is the same length as the single vertical line. It is fixed so that the naive subject is always last or last but one to give the answer. This is done 12 times, but on seven of these occasions – the critical trials – the confederates all give the same wrong

> The tendency to conformity in our society is so strong that reasonably intelligent and well-meaning young people are willing to call white black.
>
> 'Opinions and Social Pressure'

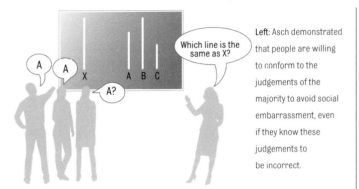

Left: Asch demonstrated that people are willing to conform to the judgements of the majority to avoid social embarrassment, even if they know these judgements to be incorrect.

answer. The key question is whether the naive subject will conform to the incorrect answer.

The results show significant levels of conformity. Despite the task being easy – mistakes are made less than 1 per cent of the time in the absence of pressure to conform – only some 20 per cent of subjects give the correct answer on every critical trial; 80 per cent conform to the majority on at least one occasion.

After conducting his experiment, Asch would ask naive students why they conformed. The majority said it was because they didn't want to appear stupid in front of their peers, while a minority said they came to the conclusion that the majority must be right. This illustrates the difference between mere compliance – going along with the majority for the sake of appearances – and internalization, where a person's judgements are affected.

> **Conformity:** A change in behaviour or thought that occurs under the pressure of social influence, normally to allow a person to fit in with a particular group.

Leon Festinger

In 1957, a book titled *A Theory of Cognitive Dissonance*, written by Leon Festinger, a young American social psychologist, was published, changing the way that psychologists think about motivation, decision-making and attitude change.

Born: 1919, New York, New York
Importance: Revolutionized the field with his cognitive dissonance theory
Died: 1989, New York, New York

Festinger's cognitive dissonance theory is built on two major claims: first, if a person simultaneously holds two or more conflicting beliefs, this will cause them discomfort; and second, this discomfort functions as a motive to reduce dissonance, which is achieved either by changing one of the beliefs or by introducing a rationalization to explain the conflict.

The phenomenon of cognitive dissonance is often illustrated with reference to a person who smokes cigarettes. If one assumes this person values their own life, then the cognition 'I smoke' is inconsistent with the cognition 'smoking is potentially lethal'. In this situation, a smoker might seek to reduce dissonance by rejecting the evidence that links smoking to cancer, or by denying that longevity is the measure of a good life, or by emphasizing the pleasure that smoking brings.

This example shows how cognitive dissonance can both shape attitudes and undermine our ability to think rationally. This carries with it certain dangers, as another oft cited example will show. Imagine it's come to your attention that a number of people in your workplace believe you have been bullying a subordinate. This results in a conflict between the cognition 'I am a good, fair-minded person' and the cognition 'people think I'm a bully'. In this situation, merely altering your behaviour will not straightforwardly eliminate the dissonance, because it leaves both cognitions in place. However, if you tell yourself that your subordinate is incompetent, then you can justify your behaviour to yourself – he deserved it – which will result in dissonance reduction. Crucially, this will likely leave the bullying behaviour in place, and indeed may well result in it being intensified.

Festinger's theory has generated a plethora of empirical work, and has been confirmed in many novel and innovative studies. For example, Aronson and Mills hypothesized that if people undergo a great deal of trouble to join a group which then turns out to be rather dull, they will experience dissonance. You don't go to a lot of trouble to join a boring group. They tested this hypothesis in an influential 1959 study.

A group of college women underwent an initiation to join a psychology study group. For some girls, the initiation was rather embarrassing, at least in 1959 terms. They had to recite a list of obscene words. For others the initiation was trivial, and for some girls there was no initiation at all. All the girls subsequently listened to a recording of a discussion being held by the group they were joining. As Aronson and Mill predicted, the girls in the Severe Initiation condition rated the discussion more highly than the girls in the control conditions.

Festinger's notion of cognitive dissonance is now common currency, being routinely referenced by political analysts, newspaper pundits and the denizens of Twitter.

Cognitive dissonance: Now known as edema, it is a feeling of distress that occurs when a person finds themself holding two contradictory beliefs (for example, 'I'm a bully', 'I'm a nice person').

Henri Tajfel

The British-based psychologist Henri Tajfel is best known for
developing a theory of social identity, which holds that people are
predisposed to divide the world up into in-groups and out-groups,
defining themselves in terms of their membership of particular
in-groups and in opposition to particular out-groups.

Born: 1919, Włocławek,
Poland
Importance: Argued we
classify the world through
group membership
Died: 1982, Oxford, England

Tajfel's groundbreaking minimal group experiments,
conducted in the early 1970s, provide strong evidence
for this general thesis. An experimental subject is given
a trivial task to complete – for example, guessing the
number of dots in a cluster – and then directed to a
cubicle, where they are told they will be required to
allocate 'points' to two other people, who will be able
to swap the points for money once the experiment is over.

The subject is then informed that they have been assigned to
a specific 'group' on the basis of how accurately they estimated
the number of dots in the cluster. They are also told to which
groups the two people to whom they will be required to allocate
points/money belong. The subject does not know the identity of
these people, has had no contact with them and knows nothing
about them. The idea here is to determine whether this kind of
minimal group membership will make a difference to the way
that subjects distribute rewards; in other words, will subjects
discriminate in favour of the people in their own group and
against non-group members.

Tajfel's results show that this is precisely what they will do.
In fact, when offered a choice, subjects seek to maximize the
difference between what is allocated to the in-group member and
what is allocated to the out-group member, even if this means the
in-group member receives less overall than would be available via an
alternative strategy.

This is a rather disconcerting result. It shows that even if we don't know the other members of our 'group', have never interacted with them, and stand to gain nothing by favouring them, we are still willing to discriminate in favour of in-group members and against out-group members.

Tajfel argues that social identity is the mechanism by which individuals orient themselves towards the society in which they exist. It is that part of an individual's self-concept which derives from their membership of a social group and from the emotional ties thereby engendered. People will tend to remain members of their social groups if the groups contribute positively to their social identity – that is, if they derive satisfaction from their group membership.

Tajfel notes that social groups become salient for members in terms of their differences from other social groups. For example, economic deprivation gains significance for a social group in terms of a comparison with other less deprived groups. Thus, a group can only become a group in the sense of having an awareness of its common characteristics and common fate when there are other groups present in the social order. In-groups define themselves in terms of out-groups.

Although Tajfel's work is not widely known outside the domain of professional psychology, there is no questioning its significance. In 1998, his former students and colleagues published the book Social Groups and Identities, as a posthumous tribute to the continuing importance of his work.

Experimental subject:
The human subjects of an experiment (so, for example, if you're testing memory, then the person whose memory you are testing is the experimental subject).

Philip Zimbardo

In a career lasting more than 40 years, the American psychologist Philip Zimbardo has conducted important research on a diverse range of topics, including attitude formation and change, post-traumatic stress syndrome, heroism and shyness. However, his career has largely been defined by a single study, the Stanford Prison Experiment, which took place in 1971.

Born: 1933, New York, New York

Importance: His Stanford Prison Experiment is a standout study in the history of psychology

The experiment was designed to explore the question of whether prison system brutality is a product of dysfunctional personalities, or whether it is caused, at least in part, by the dehumanizing nature of prison life itself. As Zimbardo put it, the issue at stake was whether people's goodness would triumph over the evil of a prison-like environment. Zimbardo created his 'prison' in the basement of the psychology laboratory at Stanford University and recruited subjects through a newspaper advertisement. Before the study began, he made sure that the chosen participants were psychologically healthy and had had no previous run-ins with the law. His subjects, all students, were randomly allocated to 'prison guard' and 'prisoner' groups, meaning that both groups were representative of young, white, middle-class America.

The results of the experiment were both stunning and dismaying. It took only a day for the guards to begin to display significant levels of aggression towards the prisoners, with the encounters between the two groups characteristically being 'negative, hostile, affrontive and dehumanizing'.

This had a large and disastrous psychological effect on the prisoners. Zimbardo reports that their behaviour became passive and 'zombie-like', and that as early as the second day, depression, rage and acute anxiety were all evident. By the time the experiment came to a premature end, after six of a planned 14 days, five

 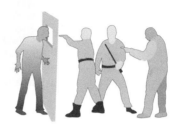

Above: Zimbardo's Stanford Prison Experiment, highlighting the prison system brutality of guards towards prisoners, is one of the most significant psychological studies, as it showed that people are predisposed to engage in negative and hostile behaviour given the presence of certain institutional and social cues.

prisoners had been released because of acute psychological suffering, and of the remaining prisoners, only two said they would not be willing to forfeit the money they had earned in return for 'parole'.

Zimbardo's prison experiment provides strong evidence that social and institutional forces can make good people do horrible things. Although the experiment has been criticized on ethical grounds, it is rightly considered one of the most significant studies in the history of psychology.

Stanley Milgram

The American social psychologist Stanley Milgram is best known for a series of classic experiments on obedience conducted in the early 1960s, which showed that under particular conditions most people are willing to torture another human being.

Born: 1933, New York, New York
Importance: Credited with discoveries in human obedience
Died: 1984, New York, New York

Milgram's first experiment, now known as the 'remote-victim' experiment, had the following set-up. Forty male experimental subjects were told they were taking part in a study that was looking at the effects of punishment on learning. Each subject was told they were going to be a 'teacher', and they were paired with an experimenter's stooge, who would play the role of 'learner'. Everything from that point on was scripted, except for the behaviour of each subject (i.e., the teacher).

The learner was put into a separate room and wired up to electrodes, through which it seemed an electric shock could be delivered each time an error was made. The teacher was given a small electric shock to convince him that the set-up was real (though it wasn't), and then went ahead with the memory test. Each time the learner made a mistake, the teacher was instructed to deliver an electric shock to the learner, with the intensity of the shock increasing by 15 volts for each subsequent mistake.

The extraordinary result of this experiment was that every teacher was willing to deliver a shock of up to 300 volts – labelled 'Intense shock' on the machine – despite the fact that it (apparently) caused the learner to pound desperately on the wall. Also, some two-thirds of subjects were willing to give the highest possible shock of 450 volts, even though by this point the learner appeared to be non-responsive.

Milgram found a similar pattern of responses across a total of 18 different experiments, comprising a total of 646 participants

Above: Milgram's shocking obedience studies demonstrated that in a laboratory setting nearly two-thirds of people are willing to torture another human being if they are instructed to do so by an authority figure.

(including 40 women, who also showed a 65 per cent obedience rate). This led Milgram to conclude that 'ordinary people simply doing their jobs, and without any particular hostility on their part, can become agents in a terrible destructive process'. Milgram also conducted other important research in a career cut short by his untimely death at the age of 51. In particular, he has been credited with introducing the idea of 'six degrees of separation' in his work on social circles.

In Sickness and in Health

Abnormal psychology is the branch of psychology that looks at aberrant patterns of thought and behaviour. In this section, we look at the work and thought of psychoanalysts such as Freud and Jung; at the medicalizing of mental illness through the work of clinicians such as Emil Kraepelin; and at the work of humanistic psychologists, such as Abraham Maslow and Carl Rogers, which led to the emergence of client-centred therapeutic techniques.

The Medical Model

We have no enemy whom we can fight, exorcise, or dispel
by 'cure'. What we do have are problems in living...

Thomas Szasz

The medical model asserts that certain patterns of abnormal
behaviour are best viewed as illnesses. The significance of this idea
for the way we view phenomena such as depression and bipolar
disorder is clear in the terminology we routinely employ: mental
illness, mental disorder and psychopathology.

It is possible to get a good idea of what's involved in the medical
model by looking at how modern psychiatry views schizophrenia,
the most severe of the common mental disorders. People with
schizophrenia suffer a severely distorted perception of reality, which
includes disordered thinking, delusions and, above all, auditory and
non-auditory hallucinations.

The standard view among psychiatrists is that the symptoms
that lead to a diagnosis of schizophrenia are, at least in part,
caused by brain dysfunction. The dopamine hypothesis suggests
that the disorder is linked to an excess of dopamine transmission,
particularly in the mesolimbic system of the brain. There is
plenty of evidence to support this hypothesis. For example, all
antipsychotic drugs work by blocking dopamine, and all drugs
that increase dopamine can cause psychosis.

However, this medical view that schizophrenia is an illness
with an underlying pathology is by no means universally endorsed.
Some radical critics of psychiatry, such as Thomas Szasz, have
suggested that schizophrenia and, more generally, mental illness
simply do not exist. Roughly, their argument is that people are
labelled as suffering from a disorder like schizophrenia in order to

'control' and 'neutralize' behaviour that is deemed to be socially unacceptable. As we'll see later in this chapter, Szasz argues that the notion of a 'mental illness' is a contradiction in terms: the mind is a non-material, non-spatial entity, so cannot be subject to the pathological changes in physiology that constitute illness.

Empirical evidence: Data which is derived from observation and measurement, and therefore, in principle, can be verified by a community of peers.

The validity of the medical model is further called into question when one considers other mental disorders. Albert Ellis, founder of rational emotive behaviour therapy, did not look for the causes of depression in an underlying brain illness but, instead, identified a number of irrational beliefs that were characteristically held by depressed people, which resulted in them viewing the world in a negative way. In these terms, therapy should not be targeted towards the brain, as would be the case if antidepressant drugs were prescribed, but rather towards challenging the irrational beliefs that result in negative perceptions and judgements.

There is no doubt the original impulse for the medical model was good. Not least, naturalizing disorders such as schizophrenia functioned to strip them of their quasi-religious baggage – so, for example, in the West at least, hearing voices is no longer seen as a sign of witchcraft. There is also persuasive empirical evidence to suggest that identifiable physiological risk factors exist for disorders such as bipolar disorder and depression. However, the extent to which it is appropriate to label disorders that are in effect 'problems in living' as 'illnesses' remains an open question.

Emil Kraepelin

The German psychiatrist Emil Kraepelin has a strong claim to being considered the founder of scientific psychiatry. In particular, the modern systems of psychiatric classification are based on the Kraepelinian view that mental disorders are distinct entities, each with its own cause, symptoms, course and terminus. Kraepelin is also notable for having written the modern era's first widely read textbook of psychiatry.

Born: 1856, Neustrelitz, Germany
Importance: Founder of scientific psychiatry
Died: 1926, Munich, Germany

Kraepelin saw the world, including the domain of mental phenomena, in naturalistic terms. For example, he did not believe in free will, arguing that human beings are just another part of the natural world. Mental phenomena, though distinct from their physical - neural, as we now know - counterparts in the brain, are closely linked, 'parallel' phenomena (to borrow Paul Hoff's terminology). This philosophical naturalism led him to the view that science is the proper mechanism for understanding the human mind, and to a sympathy with Darwinist and biological explanations.

The torment of the states of depression, which is nearly unbearable, according to the perpetually recurring statements by the patients, engenders almost in all, at least from time to time, weariness of life.

Manic-Depressive Insanity and Paranoia

Kraepelin argued that psychiatry could only put itself on a scientific footing by conducting a systematic survey of the patterns of symptoms that occur in the presence of mental distress. This, he thought, was necessary in order to identify the boundaries of specific disease manifestations, the first stage in the process of uncovering their underlying physiological pathology. On the basis of thousands of observations, Kraepelin identified two broad categories of mental disorder; dementia praecox (now known as schizophrenia), and manic-depressive psychosis (now known as bipolar disorder).

Dementia praecox (literally, 'early dementia') has a number of characteristic symptoms, the most important of which is auditory hallucinations. Disordered thought is also common, as is the sense that thoughts are being controlled or influenced by outside sources. Kraepelin had a largely pessimistic view of dementia praecox, noting that complete recovery rarely occurs.

Manic-depressive psychosis, which is characterized by alternating episodes of mania and depression, is hard to distinguish from dementia praecox in its acute phase, but is associated with a better outcome. Symptoms of mania include racing and disordered thought, elevated mood, ideas of greatness, increased sexual appetite and weight gain; symptoms of depression include torpor, slowed speech, an inability to act, feelings of guilt and weight loss.

Kraepelin's influence goes beyond the development of his dual model of psychosis. For example, he studied the effect of substances such as alcohol and caffeine on cognitive performance long before these kinds of pharmacological studies become commonplace. There were also less savory aspects to his work, not least the fact he argued that objecting to the First World War was a sign of mental illness!

Nevertheless, Kraepelin's place in the history of psychiatry is assured. The similarity of his conceptions of dementia praecox and manic-depressive psychosis to their modern equivalents – schizophrenia and bipolar disorder – is striking, and testament both to the care he took in his observations and to the impact of his work on the development of modern psychiatry.

Sigmund Freud

It would be hard to overestimate the influence of the ideas of Sigmund Freud, the father of psychoanalysis, on twentieth century thought. More than anybody else, he is responsible for undermining the view that human beings are rational decision makers, masters of their own minds and destiny.

Born: 1856, Pribor, Czech Republic
Importance: His ideas reverberate throughout twentieth century thought
Died: 1939, London, England

Freud argued that the human psyche is divided into three distinct parts: the id, which comprises a person's instincts, primarily their libidinal instincts; the ego, which is the rational, decision-making aspect of the psyche; and the superego, which is the judgemental, censorious part. The id seeks the immediate gratification of its desires. However, governed by a reality principle, the ego is required to balance the demands of the id against the requirements of living in the world. At the same time, the ego has to manage the superego, ensuring that thoughts and behaviour fall within limits that are morally acceptable from the point of view of the superego.

This situation is replete with the potential for psychic conflict. A hypervigilant superego, for example, will result in guilt, anxiety and burial of unwanted desires and memories within the unconscious. Freud claimed that these sorts of repressed conflicts have a dynamic character. Inevitably, they make their presence felt in conscious life, through dreams, slips of the tongue (parapraxes), phobias and fantasy. In a famous case study, Freud argued that the fear of horses experienced by his patient Little Hans was in fact a manifestation of his fear of his father, which was rooted in an Oedipal desire – that is, a sexual desire – for his mother, and the fact that his father was therefore a kind of love rival.

According to Freud, it is the job of the psychoanalyst to decode the messages that the unconscious sends to the conscious mind. The

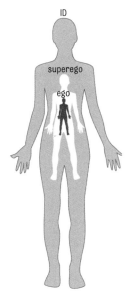

Left: Freud's psychoanalytic theory, and in particular his tripartite conception that divided the human psyche into the id, ego and superego, played a central role in the twentieth century in undermining the idea that human beings are rational social actors.

analyst will make use of techniques such as free association, word association and dream analysis in order to bring repressed memories to the surface. By knowing the unconscious roots of our thoughts and behaviour, we will be in a better position to control them.

The history of ideas of the twentieth century would have been entirely different had Freud not lived. Although there are many question marks concerning the validity of his ideas, there is no doubting his intellectual and cultural significance.

Alfred Adler

Alfred Adler, the founder of Individual Psychology and one-time colleague of Sigmund Freud, is perhaps best known in the present day as the originator of psychological concepts such as 'overcompensation' and 'the inferiority complex'.

Born: 1870, Rudolfsheim, Austria
Importance: Introduced the idea of 'overcompensation'
Died: 1937, Aberdeen, Scotland

Adler first outlined his ideas about compensation in his book, *A Study of Organic Inferiority and Its Psychical Compensation*, published in 1907. In essence, his argument was that the existence of a physiological defect – for example, deafness – will often result in a compensatory impulse that will lead an individual to excel in precisely the area most relevant to their handicap. So, for example, he noted that the ancient Greek statesman Demosthenes stuttered as a youth, but overcame this problem to become a great orator..

In his later work, Adler extended this idea so that it did not require the existence of a physiological defect. He argued that all children experience feelings of inferiority. These might be particularly pronounced in the case of a neglected, or abused, child, but even in the best circumstances, a child will feel small and helpless in the face of the adult world. The consequence is that from an early age, children are striving for power and superiority in order to compensate for these feelings of inferiority.

The neurotic response to this situation will see the child withdrawing from the world, thereby avoiding those situations that threaten to bring to light their perceived inferiority. If this is not resolved going into adulthood, then an Inferiority Complex is the likely consequence. This typically involves the adult setting impossible to accomplish 'fictive goals' and then explaining their failure to meet these goals in terms of the symptoms of their neurotic state.

Adler did not believe that a feeling of inferiority is pathological in itself. In fact, it is a normal part of development for individuals to strive for power and superiority. However, this striving must be realistic in terms of the challenges of society, work and sex, otherwise the risk of overcompensation – for example, the weak man who becomes a bully – or a retreat into neurotic illness looms large.

Adler's 'individual psychology' insists on the unity of the individual, holding that the individual traits of a personality can only be understood in terms of the unified whole. He argued that personality is fundamentally goal-oriented and that if you know the goal of a person you know in a general way what they will do.

More radically, he claimed that in the absence of the perception of some goal, thinking, feeling, willing and acting are impossible. As he put it, we would be unintegrated and in every aspect of our physiognomy, in every personal touch, similar to organisms of the rank of the amoeba. These ideas lead on to the central rule of the practice of individual psychology: 'as soon as the goal of a psychic movement or its life-plan has been recognized, then we are to assume that all the movements of its constituent parts will coincide with both the goal and the life-plan'.

Inferiority: The feeling, often unwarranted, that one is inadequate, not measuring up to society's standards across particular dimensions (for example, moral, social, intellectual).

Carl Gustav Jung

Carl Gustav Jung, the Swiss psychotherapist and founder of analytical psychology, was at one time a close friend and colleague of Sigmund Freud; however, in 1913, their friendship came to an end, in part because Jung wanted to take psychoanalytic theory in a direction that Freud had not envisaged. In particular, Jung denied that the libido is entirely sexual in character, and, therefore, contrary to Freudian orthodoxy, he believed that there was more to neurosis than simply the existence of unconscious sexual conflicts.

Born: 1875, Kesswil, Switzerland
Importance: Founder of analytical psychology
Died: 1961, Zurich, Switzerland

According to Jung, the psyche is split into three interacting parts: consciousness; the personal unconscious; and the collective unconscious. The conscious mind is the part of the psyche that is directly known to the person. Jung identified two personality types that determine how an individual is oriented towards the world. The extrovert directs libidinal energies outward towards the external world; the introvert looks inward, focusing on subjective feelings and experience. It was Jung's belief that most individuals will stay true to their personality type throughout their life.

...there is good reason for supposing that the archetypes are the unconscious images of the instincts themselves, in other words, that they are *patterns of instinctual behaviour*.

> *The Archetypes and the Collective Unconscious Pressure*

Jung's treatment of the unconscious aspects of the psyche, and particularly his idea of the collective unconscious, was unorthodox. He argued that humans are wired up to

experience and orient themselves towards the world in the same way as their ancestors did. The innate organizing principles of the collective unconscious are termed 'archetypes'. Examples include: the persona – the face we present to the world; the shadow – the source of our animal instincts; the self – the organizing principle by means of which we structure our personality; the anima – the feminine in the masculine, and the animus – the masculine in the feminine.

Although this notion of the collective unconscious is the most novel aspect of Jung's approach, it is also the most problematic. His critics contend, with some justification, that it has more in common with mythology than with scientific theory.

Jung's ideas certainly represent an interesting variation on the theme of Freudian psychoanalysis, and there is no doubting the influence of his formulations. However, the extent to which his ideas are justified by what we know about the world is questionable. This is the general case with psychoanalytic theory.

Melanie Klein

Melanie Klein was one of the pioneering figures of psychoanalysis, responsible for advances in both clinical practice and psychoanalytic theory. In particular, she devised a method for analyzing the play of children, which made it possible for psychoanalytic techniques to be applied to infants as young as two years old; and on the theoretical side, she developed an alternative treatment of the origins of the Freudian superego, and elaborated concepts such as the paranoid-schizoid position and the depressive position that are now part of the psychoanalytic lexicon.

Born: 1882, Vienna, Austria
Importance: Developed theory and clinical practice for child psychoanalysis
Died: 1960, London, England

According to orthodox Freudian theory, the superego develops with the resolution of the Oedipus complex at about four years of age. Klein rejected this view, arguing instead that its origins can be found much earlier, in the first months of life.

The earliest stages of an infant's psychic life are characterized by the existence of two major developmental phases: the paranoid-schizoid position and the depressive position. Klein's famous distinction between 'good breast' and 'bad breast' will shed some light on the character of the paranoid-schizoid position.

In the first stages of life, an infant makes no distinction between their own ego and the objects of the outside world. This means that whenever feelings of love and hatred are experienced, they are projected into the outside world, with the consequence that the objects of

> One of the many interesting and surprising experiences of the beginner in child analysis is to find in even very young children a capacity for insight which is often far greater than that of adults.
>
> *Cognitive Therapy of Depression*

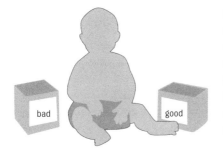

Left: Klein argued that the newly born infant experiences the world in a radically divided way, with the objects of its experience being split into those that are wholly good and those that are wholly bad.

the world take on the guise of these emotions. Thus, Klein argued that 'the earliest experiences of the infant are split between wholly good ones with "good" objects and wholly bad experiences with "bad" objects'.

The infant's first object is the mother's breast, which is sometimes rewarding (when it supplies plentiful milk) and sometimes not (when it doesn't satisfy the infant's needs). The consequence is that the infant will split their feelings of love and hatred, and project them onto a single object (the breast), thereby dividing it into two: the good breast (or mother) is loved and felt to be nourishing; the bad breast (or mother) is hated and felt to be persecutory.

The fact that the emotions of love and hate function in this all or nothing way means that the infant's world during these early months is 'peopled by gods and devils – a world which appears sometimes a heaven and at other times a very hell' (J.A.C. Brown).

Anna Freud

Anna Freud, Sigmund Freud's youngest daughter, was a renowned
clinical psychoanalyst in her own right, pioneering the practice
of child psychoanalysis and making important contributions to
psychoanalytic theory, particularly in relation to what is known
as 'ego psychology', the branch of psychoanalysis that
focuses on the normal and pathological development
of the ego or conscious mind.

Born: 1895, Vienna, Austria
Importance: Significant
figure in ego psychology
Died: 1982, London, England

In her most important work, *Ego and the Mechanisms
of Defence*, she examines the way that the ego defends
itself against the 'painful or unendurable ideas or
affects' that exist as a result of tensions between the
clamours of the id (the instinctual part of the personality), the
demands of the outside world and the prohibitions of the superego
(the moral, censorious part of the psyche).

She identifies five novel defence mechanisms: denial in fantasy,
denial in word and act, restriction of the ego, identification with
the aggressor and altruism.

Denial in fantasy refers to the process of managing a painful
fact or situation by imaginatively transforming it into its opposite.
For example, a child whose mother has died might fantasize that
she is still alive, on some fantastical journey, and will one day
return to her family.

Denial in word and deed similarly refers to the process of
denying some aspect of the world, only this time through words
and actions. A young boy who fears losing the love of his father,
and who would like the occasional cuddle, but doesn't want to
admit this to himself, might tell himself that he hates his father and
that his father is mean.

Restriction of the ego is illustrated by the case of the small boy
who refuses to play football with his friends because he recognizes

their superior skills and fears humiliation. His reluctance to play the game then extends into a general dislike for the game and a disdain for those people who choose to play and follow it.

Identification with the aggressor is a method of dealing with anxiety that relies on adopting the characteristics of the oppressor, thereby transforming oneself into the powerful figure. For example, the boy bullied at home by his father might himself bully weaker children at school; or the child bullied at school, might bully his younger siblings.

Altruism functions as a defence mechanism by allowing the cathartic fulfilment of desire by the surrender of one's own wishes to another person. Anna Freud points to the example of Cyrano de Bergerac, who helps a rival win the affections of the woman he himself loves because he believes his own ugliness denies him 'the dream of being loved'.

Psyche: The totality of the human mind, both conscious and unconscious (this term is often used in the context of psychoanalytic theory).

Although Anna Freud rose to prominence in part because she was the daughter of Sigmund Freud, there is no doubt she made important and novel contributions in her own right, particularly in her commitment to improving the lives of children suffering because of a broken-down relationship with their parents.

Carl Rogers

The American psychologist Carl Rogers was one of the early pioneers of the humanistic approach to psychology, and the driving force behind the development of client-centred psychotherapy. He was also nominated for the Nobel Peace Prize in 1987 for his work on intergroup conflict in Northern Ireland and South Africa.

Born: 1902, Oak Park, Ilinois
Importance: Pioneered humanistic psychology and won the Nobel Peace Prize
Died: 1987, San Diego, California

At the centre of Rogers' approach is the concept of 'the self', which refers to an 'organized, consistent set of perceptions and beliefs about oneself'. Put simply, the self, or self-concept, is the mental picture that a person has of themselves. If this picture is reasonably accurate, if it is congruent with reality, then it will fit well with actual experience. However, if it is not, if it is incongruent with reality, then the lack of fit between self-concept and actual experience can lead to psychological difficulties.

We think we listen, but very rarely do we listen with real understanding, true empathy. Yet listening, of this very special kind, is one of the most potent forces for change that I know.

'A Way of Being'

According to Rogers, incongruent experiences threaten the integrity of a person's self-concept, and therefore provoke anxiety. The typical response is to employ defence mechanisms in order to deal with the incongruence. For example, a young woman who considers herself unattractive, but is asked to a dance by an attractive man, might explain away the incongruence by telling herself that he only feels sorry for her, or that it is a joke. In this way, she protects her self-concept, but only at the expense of denying herself a potentially positive experience.

Rogers advocated client-centred therapy as the means to deal with incongruence. This relies on what he called unconditional positive regard. The therapist provides complete acceptance and nonjudgemental support of the client as a person in a setting that is genuinely emotionally supportive and engaged. The aim is to allow the client to come to terms with thoughts and feelings they would otherwise deny as being their own, thereby enabling them to develop a more realistic self-concept.

Rogers identified six conditions that had to be met for this therapeutic outcome to occur. (1) The therapist must operate on the principle that the individual is responsible for themselves. (2) The therapist needs to accept that the client has a strong drive to become mature, independent and well-adjusted, and rely on this drive for therapeutic change. (3) The therapist must cultivate a warm and accepting atmosphere. (4) Appropriate limits in the therapeutic setting are always limits on behavior not attitudes or thoughts. (5) The therapist must demonstrate acceptance, which involves neither approval nor disapproval, based on a deep understanding of the attitudes expressed by the client; (6) The therapist must not blame, advise, accuse or probe.

According to Rogers, if these conditions are met the client will 'arrive at a clearer conscious realization of his motivating attitudes and will accept himself more completely', and therefore choose new goals that are more satisfying than the previous maladjusted goals.

Humanistic psychology:
An approach to psychology that emphasizes the importance of human experience, the potential for personal growth, and the possibility of self-fulfilment.

Abraham Maslow

The American psychologist Abraham H. Maslow was one
of the most important figures in the humanistic psychology
movement that emerged in the United States in the middle part
of the twentieth century. The humanistic approach, in contrast
to behaviourism and psychoanalysis, emphasizes the
importance of human experience, the potential for
personal growth and the possibility of self-fulfilment.

Born: 1908, Brooklyn,
New York
Importance: Foremost in
humanistic psychology
Died: 1970, Menlo Park,
California

According to Maslow, human motivation can be
understood in terms of a pyramidal hierarchy of
needs. At the bottom, there are basic physiological
needs; then come higher level needs, including safety
needs, the need for love and belonging, and the need
for esteem. At the top there is the need for self-actualization,
which refers to the possibility of realizing one's full potential, or
'becoming everything that one is capable of becoming'.

Normally, needs at the bottom must be satisfied before higher
level needs come into play. For example, a starving person will
not be concerned with their need for esteem until their hunger has
been satisfied. At the higher levels, needs are not merely a matter of
satisfying biological imperatives, but rather are dependent upon
living life in a certain kind of way, and, therefore, they are much
harder to satisfy.

Even though everybody is capable of self-actualization, most
people do not achieve it. Maslow identified William James, Albert
Einstein and Abraham Lincoln as example of self-actualizers,
arguing that they had in common that they were spontaneous
in action and thought, able to perceive reality accurately, happy
to tolerate uncertainty, creative, interested in problem solving
and able to enjoy deep relationships with just a small number of
people. Maslow also noted that self-actualizers seem to have many

Above: Maslow specified a pyramidal hierarchy of needs, according to which needs at the bottom – for example, for food – must be satisfied before higher level needs – for example, for love and belonging – come into play.

peak experiences in their lives. These are moments of extreme happiness and fulfilment, which often involve a loss of the sense of self, and which will sometimes result in positive changes to a person's behaviour.

It not yet clear whether the kinds of ideas pioneered by Maslow have been particularly effective in helping people to achieve psychological health. However, humanistic psychology has been an important corrective to the scientism of behaviourist psychology and the reductionism of psychoanalysis.

Albert Ellis

The American psychologist Albert Ellis spent the early part of his career committed to the methods of psychoanalysis as the deepest and most effective form of therapy. However, his confidence in the technique evaporated at the beginning of the 1950s, which led him to develop **Rational Emotive Behavioural Therapy** (REBT), the therapeutic approach for which he is now celebrated.

Born: 1913, Pittsburgh, Pennsylvania
Importance: Introduced an original form of therapy
Died: 2007, New York, New York

REBT holds that psychological problems arise from irrational judgements and interpretations; from inappropriate emotional reactions to unexceptional stimuli; and from habitually dysfunctional patterns of behaviour.

According to Ellis, if something unpleasant occurs in a person's life, they are confronted with a choice: they can either be healthily and self-helpingly frustrated, disappointed and annoyed; or they can be unhealthily and self-defeatingly inconsolable, terrified and panicked. Normally, the healthy response is engendered by rational beliefs and the unhealthy response by irrational or self-defeating beliefs.

Ellis identified a number of irrational and self-defeating beliefs that are common in Western and other cultures. These include, for example: 'I must be loved and accepted by absolutely everybody'; 'I must always be excellent and never make mistakes'; 'I must damn others if they behave in ways I consider wicked'. More generally, Ellis argued that when people take their strong desire for love, success and comfort, and turn it into a series of musts, needs and imperatives, then it is likely they will end up anxious, depressed and self-pitying.

The goal of REBT is to teach people to challenge their own irrational and self-defeating ideas and beliefs. Therefore, effective therapists not only listen carefully to their clients, and provide unconditional acceptance whatever their clients' circumstances, but they also show them how and why their thinking goes wrong, and what they can do to change their thoughts and behaviour in a way that will lessen their psychological distress.

Therapy tends to extend beyond the confines of the formal therapeutic setting, often involving homework to be completed by the client. This will sometimes mean the client will be asked to put themselves into situations that make them uncomfortable, allowing them to challenge the irrational thoughts that occur as a result. For example, the client with social phobia might be required to make a fool of themselves in public, with the aim of demonstrating that nothing terrible will happen as a result. In this sense, REBT is a much more active-directive therapy than more traditional psychotherapies, which, according to Ellis, accounts for its greater effectiveness.

Rational Emotive Behavioural Therapy (REBT):
A form of therapy that aims to change patients' thought patterns in order to reduce psychological distress. It rests on the belief that the way we think affects the way we feel and how we behave.

There is no doubting that Ellis's ideas have had a tremendous impact on the profession of psychotherapy. In a 1982 article in American Psychologist, Darrell Smith reported on the results of a survey of more than 400 professional psychologists which aimed to discover the then current trends in counselling and psychotherapy. Albert Ellis was second only to Carl Rogers in terms of his influence.

Thomas Szasz

In the late 1950s, the Hungarian-born, American-based psychiatrist Thomas Szasz wrote a number of articles critical of the practice of psychiatry, arguing in one that the notion of mental illness had no more validity as an explanation of behaviour than the claim that a person had been possessed by the devil. These articles were a prelude to the publication of his seminal work, *The Myth of Mental Illness,* which can be seen as an attempt to demolish the conceptual foundations of psychiatry.

Born: 1920, Budapest, Hungary
Importance: Rethinking the foundations of psychiatry
Died: 2012, Manlius, New York

According to Szasz, the claim that mental illnesses are diagnosable brain disorders is either a lie or a naive error. The concept of 'illness' requires the presence of a pathological change in cells, tissues and organs, which is clearly impossible in the case of a non-spatial, non-material entity such as the mind. It follows that the idea of 'mental illness' is merely a metaphor, and 'minds can be "sick": only in the sense that jokes are "sick" or economies are "sick"'. Szasz did not deny that, in some cases, the symptoms of 'mental illness' are caused by the presence of an organic brain disease (as in the case of Alzheimer's disease, for example). However, in these cases, the patient doesn't have a mental illness at all, they have a physical illness, and to claim otherwise is simply to misdiagnose them.

Szasz argued that in the vast majority of cases of 'mental illness', there is no underlying brain disease. Rather, what is being diagnosed as 'mental illness' are 'problems in living', forms of behaviour that deviate from what society considers to be acceptable. In this sense, a diagnosis of 'mental illness' is an attempt to control behaviour that is potentially threatening to the social order. Thus, he insisted that 'mental hospitals are like prisons, not hospitals; that involuntary mental hospitalization is a type of imprisonment, not medical care; and that coercive psychiatrists function as judges and jailers, not healers'.

Not surprisingly, these arguments provoked considerable controversy. Martin Roth, for example, pointed out that if an inability to specify an underlying pathological state means a disease doesn't exist, then epilepsy wasn't an organic disorder when first described by Hippocrates in the 5th Century BCE, and only became so in the nineteenth century. Similarly, Parkinsonism, despite being accurately described by James Parkinson in 1817, only becomes a disease shortly before the First World War when lesions were discovered in the corpus striatum.

Szasz's rhetoric has also come under fire. Alan Stone, in a critical assessment of Szasz's work written while Szasz's reputation was at its highest, commented sardonically that it was quite hard for psychiatrists to think of themselves as modern-day Dominicans and grand inquisitors despite Szasz's seemingly serious contention that 'institutional psychiatry is the continuation of the Inquisition. All that has really changed is the vocabulary and the social styles'.

Szasz accepted that the behaviour patterns that psychiatrists identify as indicative of mental illness are often strange, unnerving and annoying. They may also be upsetting to the person involved. But, in almost all cases, they are not a symptom of a brain disorder.

Aaron Beck

The American psychiatrist Aaron Beck is best known as the originator of cognitive therapy, an approach widely used in the treatment of clinical depression that stresses the importance of the way that individuals view themselves and the world around them for an understanding of the condition.

Born: 1921, Providence, Rhode Island
Importance: Pioneered cognitive therapy used in treating clinical depression

Beck's crucial insight was that patients who are depressed view many of their circumstances in an unrealistically negative light, and that it is the constant repetition of negative thoughts that keeps painful emotions and problematic behaviours in place.

His cognitive triad specifies three types of negative thoughts that are common in depression: thoughts about the self, the world and the future. People suffering from depression often see themselves as useless or hopeless, and view the world as unfriendly, hostile and alien, confronting them with insurmountable barriers and obstacles. They see no way out of their situation and view the future through a prism of hopelessness.

Beck argues that the automatic negative thoughts characteristic of depression arise from a number of typical cognitive biases, including, for example, black and white thinking, and arbitrary inference. Black and white thinking is most commonly associated with the setting of impossible goals, which, when not met, result in an inappropriately negative judgement. For example, an athlete trains hard to run a marathon, but aims for a hugely unlikely time, and then is highly critical of himself when he fails to meet his target.

Arbitrary inference occurs when an individual draws an inappropriately negative conclusion on the basis of insufficient or absent evidence. For example, a woman concludes that she is hopeless because she happens to wear the same dress to a party as a friend.

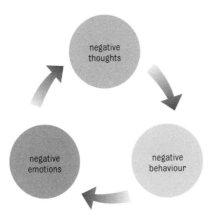

Above: Beck is the originator of cognitive therapy, a therapeutic technique that not only emphasizes the importance of negative thoughts in the emergence of disorders but also the repetitive nature of said negative thoughts that keep negative emotions and behaviour in circulation.

Cognitive therapy aims to challenge these sorts of negative thoughts and cognitive biases. With the help of a therapist, clients are taught how to subject their judgements to reality testing. In this way, the hope is they will come to see just how inappropriately negative their thoughts actually are.

Robin Murray

The Scottish psychiatrist Sir Robin Murray earned his reputation as one of the world's top psychiatrists primarily through his work with schizophrenia patients. Together with his colleagues, he originated and developed the idea that schizophrenia is at least in part a neurodevelopmental disorder.

Born: 1944, Glasgow, Scotland
Importance: Argued schizophrenia is partly a neurodevelopmental disorder

The orthodox view about schizophrenia used to be that it is a degenerative disorder. The brain of a schizophrenia sufferer starts off normal, but something happens to it during their teens or twenties, and then it deteriorates.

Murray's idea is different. He proposes that the brains of people with schizophrenia have developed in subtly deviant ways. Put simply, something has happened to the wiring of the brain – perhaps for reasons to do with genetics or early environmental insult – that makes the schizophrenia sufferer more vulnerable to hallucinations and delusions. It is important to be clear about what Murray is claiming here. It is *not* that particular developmental problems lead inevitably to schizophrenia. Rather, it is that under certain circumstances, neural systems develop in a way that makes the occurrence of schizophrenia more likely. In particular, subtle developmental changes leave people much more vulnerable to the effects of stressful events in their lives.

Murray's work with Afro-Caribbean patients sheds light on the complexity of the causal factors that result in schizophrenia. He found that rates of schizophrenia among people of Afro-Caribbean origin living in the UK are six times higher than among the white population in the UK, and, crucially, six times higher than among the black population living in the West Indies. This suggests that if these patients had still been living in the West

Indies, they would have been far less likely to have developed the illness. Murray suggests that there is something about the adversity in the lives of this group of people that explains the much higher incidence rate.

In the 1960s, an anti-psychiatry movement emerged which held that mental disorders such as schizophrenia don't exist as distinct biological entities, but rather are best seen as patterns of behaviour designed to manage the conflicting demands of a sick society.

Murray rejects this radical claim that mental illnesses, including schizophrenia, are entirely caused by social factors. There are differences between the brains of schizophrenics and non-schizophrenics, and there is an inherited component to the disorder. Nevertheless, he has sympathy with the impulse that led to anti-psychiatry. He criticizes the conditions that psychiatric patients often face as in-patients, arguing that society doesn't care enough about the mentally ill to ensure they get effective treatment in reasonable surroundings.

However, Murray does believe that things have got better over the last 50 years for people suffering from mental illnesses. Many of his patients do very well, using a combination of antipsychotic drugs and psychological therapy to allow them to live full lives, often working successfully in a professional capacity.

Schizophrenia:
A psychiatric condition, caused by a mixture of genetics and environmental factors, that changes behaviour and thoughts, leading to the development of any of the following symptoms: delusions, hallucinations, social withdrawal and a lack of emotion.